INTEGRATING RETAIL FINANCIAL MARKETS IN EUROPE
BETWEEN UNCERTAINTIES & CHALLENGES

RYM AYADI

CENTRE FOR EUROPEAN POLICY STUDIES
BRUSSELS

The Centre for European Policy Studies (CEPS) is an independent policy research institute in Brussels. Its mission is to produce sound policy research leading to constructive solutions to the challenges facing Europe.

This report has benefited from discussions that took place within the CEPS-ECRI Task Force on "The internal market for retail financial services: Much remains to be done", which met from October 2005 to April 2007. The Task Force was chaired by Anton van Rossum, former CEO of Fortis. A list of the institutions and organisations that participated in the discussions appears in the final appendix. The report has also benefited from the meetings and position papers of the FIN-USE Expert Forum of Financial Services Users set up by the European Commission, in which the author served as a member from June 2007 to June 2010, as well as internal research conducted by CEPS.

Dr Rym Ayadi is a Senior Research Fellow and Head of the Financial Institutions and Prudential Policy research unit at CEPS. She wishes to thank Emrah Arbak and Willem Pieter de Groen for their excellent research assistance. The views expressed are attributable solely to the author in a personal capacity and not to any institution with which she is associated nor to the participants of the Task Force or the FIN-USE Expert Forum of Financial Services Users.

ISBN 978-94-6138-084-5

Centre for European Policy Studies
Place du Congrès 1, B-1000 Brussels
Tel: (32.2) 229.39.11 • Fax: (32.2) 219.41.51
Website: www.ceps.eu; E-mail: info@ceps.eu

CONTENTS

EXECUTIVE SUMMARY AND CONCLUSIONS

The financial crisis has damaged consumer confidence in the financial services market. Trillions of losses in euros and government bailouts have partly been born by taxpayers, small investors and retail customers in several member states. In such circumstances, in order to continue the construction of the internal market for retail financial services, European policy-makers ought to rethink their approach to financial market integration and respond to the challenges that lie ahead in ensuring financial safety for retail consumers and enhancing consumer protection at the EU level. To do so, European frameworks for financial safety, regulation and consumer protection are necessary to restore market and consumer confidence in retail financial services.

- An integrated and competitive market in retail financial services is only viable if it is efficient, stable and inclusive, and if it provides an optimal level of protection for the public at the domestic and cross-border levels. A new Financial Services Action Plan (FSAP) post-crisis must reconsider the objectives and the means of its predecessor, the 1999 FSAP, which was the blueprint for the construction of the internal market for financial services. The new FSAP must consider the appropriate lessons from the crisis and be aligned with the new philosophy of the 2020 European agenda for sustainable and inclusive growth.

- The single market in financial services requires a European solution with regard to deposit insurance to safeguard and restore the confidence of individual depositors. Such a scheme would in principle be a more efficient solution than the currently fragmented framework of almost 40 deposit guarantee schemes in the 27 member states. It would also help remove competitive distortions, deal with administrative burdens, avoid confusion for the customers of branch/subsidiaries and most importantly promote the internal market for retail banking.

- Implementing and enforcing existing directives in the retail financial market area, will not only help to achieve the regulatory coherence and convergence necessary for retail market integration, but also help to ensure market confidence. Regulation must be enforced, as is the case for competition policy. Competition authorities have the power to levy substantial fines on market participants who breach competition law. Similarly, regulation needs to be complemented by a credible system of sanctions if rules are breached. The role of the new European Supervisory Authorities is paramount to achieving this.

- Consumers and investors must have access to the necessary and relevant information on all retail financial products supplied by financial services providers in the 27 member states to allow them to make informed, effective choices and decisions. If access to information is to be effective as a policy tool, it is important that the information disclosed to consumers is easily available, consistent, easily understandable and comparable, and that it covers the *risks*, *costs*, *features*, *terms and conditions*, and *redress* associated with the product and service. As soon as regulatory and consumer policy frameworks are maximally harmonised, an observatory of retail financial services should be established to improve transparency and ensure comparability among products and services.

- On the supply side, financial institutions, advisers/intermediaries and other players should be required to operate with a generally high duty of care in assessing consumers' needs and level of financial sophistication, so that appropriate advice and recommendations are given. Mis-selling, unduly high prices, unfair commercial practices and the provision of improper information to customers must be banned and legally sanctioned. An annual consumer satisfaction barometer should be part of the strategies of financial providers and must become part of their annual reports.

- All in all, an EU ethical code of conduct should be agreed and enforced by the profession in close consultation with consumer organisations. Responsibility for enforcing the code should be taken by the boards. Consumer satisfaction is as important as that of other stakeholders. Furthermore, the Commission should produce clear guidelines about i) consumer needs assessments (for example, information gathering, transparency level and adequacy of financial services) and ii) recognised professional standards to ensure that intermediaries/advisers apply consistently high standards in their domestic and cross-border services. The interests of end-users of financial services (consumers, pensioners, small enterprises, retail investors and so forth) must be better represented at the EU level. It is therefore critical that the EU increases the resources available to advocates of end-users and develops ideas on how to create a more level playing field during the policy-making process in future.

- Capacity-building could be complemented by the creation of a European consumer protection agency in the medium term when evidence of more retail financial market integration is apparent. Its mandate would be to protect European end-users from deceptive practices by the financial industry and to enforce relevant regulations in retail financial services. The agency should be funded under the EU's budget.

INTRODUCTION

Since the opening of capital accounts in 1988, the introduction of the 'single passport' for investment firms in 1993 and the establishment of the euro in 1999, the integration of both wholesale and retail financial markets has been a European priority. Although the liberalisation of capital movements and the elimination of currency barriers have helped bring markets together, partly achieving a single market for the wholesale segment, market integration for retail financial services remains elusive. The most fundamental reason is that financial products reflect the legal, tax and regulatory systems under which they are executed and these systems differ widely across Europe. The integration process in financial services is founded on the interaction between minimum harmonisation, mutual recognition and home country control. Such principles have often produced mixed results because of the major obstacles they have encountered.[1]

Adopted in 1999, the FSAP served as the blueprint for establishing a common regulatory framework for Europe's financial markets. But it has been far more ambitious to achieve an integrated wholesale market than is the case for retail. The FSAP aimed at creating a single, integrated wholesale market for financial services and a secure and open retail market in Europe. This was regarded as critical for providing individuals with the best savings opportunities and for giving companies access to 'deep and

---

[1] Minimum harmonisation can lead to indefinite negotiation processes, which often result in watering down the main provisions and which leave room for national discretion. Mutual recognition has its virtues and deficiencies, but in practice it is hard to satisfy home and host country supervisors, particularly when the subsidiarity principle ought to be respected. Home country control can work when institutions enter into a foreign market through a branch but not through a subsidiary.

liquid markets for raising capital'. More specifically, a single wholesale market would allow corporate borrowers to raise capital on an EU-wide basis and give investors and intermediaries access to all markets from a single point of entry. At the same time, an open retail market would remove the barriers to the provision of cross-border retail services and give retail customers the information and assurance required to access services on an EU-wide basis. Much was achieved under the FSAP up to the 2005 target date for implementation. The FSAP was followed by a White Paper on financial services policy, which outlined the Commission's policy priorities for 2005–10. Besides emphasising the importance of finalising, consolidating and implementing past initiatives, as well as promoting better regulation and increased transparency, the White Paper launched a set of new initiatives in retail financial services, which are examined in this report. Until a few years ago, economic and market evidence suggested that European financial integration was underway in many sectors, particularly wholesale markets, stock exchanges, and clearing and settlement. Conversely the market for retail financial services for individuals and small and medium-sized enterprises (SMEs) have remained highly fragmented and scattered across national frontiers. Since the eruption of the 2007–09 financial crisis, fundamental regulatory changes have been in the pipeline. The internal market for financial services, which was introduced a decade ago, was caught unprepared for the 'financequake'. The foundations of modern finance have been shaken and several years of internal market construction have been put to a serious test, highlighting the limits and risks entailed in the absence of a credible and functioning cross-border safety net, and the ineffectiveness of consumer protection rules.

The purpose of this report is to assess the state of play and to summarise the main challenges in the wake of the crisis to building a genuine market for retail financial services within the EU. The ultimate goal is to both advance the Europe 2020 strategy and achieve an integrated, efficient, competitive, stable and inclusive financial market. The analysis focuses on those areas where integration is most limited: the retail financial services markets for individuals and SMEs. This report is structured as follows: Chapter 1 provides a general diagnosis of the situation and the remaining obstacles to integration in the retail financial market. Chapter 2 analyses the key market and policy achievements in payments, retail credit and investment markets. Chapter 3 addresses the main challenges ahead.

1. General Diagnosis

This chapter examines the state of integration of retail financial markets in Europe, the main obstacles hindering the development of an integrated market and the links between financial integration, competition, efficiency, stability and inclusion.

1.1 What is an integrated market and how is it measured?

The theory of market integration in its simplest form is characterised by the 'law of one price'. Broadly speaking, this means that when inter-market trading starts, observed differentials in the prices of commodities and services will tend to reduce and eventually disappear given the absence of any abnormal shocks to the system and the existence of individuals' capability and willingness to engage in arbitrage.[2] Additionally, the definition of integration adopted by the European Commission (2005a) in its *Financial Integration Monitor 2005* has been taken as a reference point: "Financial integration is a process, driven by market forces, in which separate national financial markets gradually enter into competition with each other and eventually become one financial market, characterised by converging prices, product supply and converging efficiency/profitability among the financial services providers."

As pointed out in the European Commission's definition, financial integration is a process, and dynamic by nature. It can be driven by EU policies that seek convergence and remove obstacles but also by broader market trends, including technological developments, communications and financial innovation.

---

[2] The one price law is based on a strong assumption that transaction costs are neglected (Kleimeier and Sander, 2007).

Empirically, market integration is difficult to assess, as there is not yet a single accepted standard of measurement that encompasses a complete set of parameters driving integration in financial services. Academic literature has mainly focused on two types of measurement: the law of one price and quantity-based measures.

Based on the law of one price, it is possible to derive measures of integration. For example, the cross-sectional dispersion of relevant variables (such as interest rate spreads or asset return differentials) can be used as an indicator of integration. Yet, it is maintained that the law of one price has a number of limits in practice because prices and specifically interest rates with respect to retail banking remain different among European member states, even for identical products. This is more likely owing to the extent of competition and the high degree of differentiation of products and services within the banking sector. Moreover, the reasoning behind prices neglects the underlying risks, such as differences in products, quality, efficiency and profitability. Accordingly, from the price-based assessment, only the risk-adjusted returns should be equal.[3] But, as suggested by Adam et al. (2002) and then applied by the European Commission in its annual *Financial Integration Monitor* reports, the convergence of retail interest rates remains an accurate indicator of integration. For instance, if national interest rates react similarly to shocks in common factors, this could be perceived as co-movement over time, which suggests co-integration.

The discrepancy in the average price for day-to-day banking services can also be used as an indicator of the EU's retail market integration. It is calculated as the standard deviation of a region's bank prices divided by the region's average price.[4]

Apart from price comparisons, other quantity-based indicators are used to measure integration. These indicators directly assess the extent of cross-border flows (the number and value of mergers & acquisitions (M&As), volume of cross-border loans and deposits, etc.). Still, cross-border

---

[3] See Flood and Rose (2004) for an illustration of this methodology to measure financial integration and the annual *Financial Integration Monitor* reports of the European Commission (2004a, 2005a, 2006a) for the application of this methodology to financial market integration.

[4] A minor discrepancy means that a region's prices are close to the average and relatively homogeneous, while a larger discrepancy indicates that price levels vary greatly among banks in a region.

M&As are neither a necessary nor a sufficient condition for an integrated banking market. The absence of cross-border M&As can in fact signal the existence of an integrated market when integrated money or bond markets equalise the banks' cost of funds and when competition ensures pricing based on these marginal costs. In such a market, there would be no motivation for cross-border M&As (Kleimeier and Sander, 2007).

Furthermore, financial integration can be assessed by applying the concepts of convergence towards an EU-wide and/or best practice. Evidence of this can be found by estimating the convergence of cost efficiency derived from applying stochastic frontier analysis methodology (see for instance, Casu and Girardone, 2002, 2007; and Weill, 2009) or profit efficiency derived from parametric and non-parametric models. The speed at which markets are integrating can additionally be assessed by using the concept of β-convergence.[5]

Finally, macroeconomic indicators can be used to assess integration, such as the correlation between investment and savings within a country and the cross-border country correlations in consumption growth. To the extent that macroeconomic series are volatile, their use in relation to the integration of retail banking is undermined and need to be complemented by other indicators.

No matter what the standard measurement is, the interpretation of market integration evidence should take into account other parameters, i.e. the convergence of regulations, removal of obstacles, harmonisation of pricing and so on, along with the types of financial service activities and the business models of the institutions (wholesale versus retail, proximity versus international, etc.).

All in all, market integration is not an end in itself. The ultimate goal for an internal market for retail financial services is to establish a market that is efficient, competitive, stable and inclusive.

1.2 State of market integration and main remaining obstacles

In recent years, a number of factors have driven a modest progress in the integration of the retail financial market. These factors range from the introduction of the euro, the single monetary policy and new distribution

---

[5] The *β-coefficient* is the estimated coefficient of a regression where the change in the spread between a specific country's interest rate and the benchmark is regressed on the lagged spread.

channels (such as the Internet) for the provision of financial services, to EU passports and home country control. Notwithstanding these drivers, the retail business remains confined to national borders. The main reason is that retail consumers are naturally scattered spatially[6] and have little mobility, which is in stark contrast to the wholesale sector.

The empirical evidence[7] on the degree of banking integration in Europe has not been very conclusive, although there seems to be agreement that more integration in financial services can be observed in the new member states (NMS).[8]

In what follows, we summarise the key results from the empirical evidence derived from price and quantity indicators and we assess the remaining obstacles that need to be tackled in the future.

Evidence derived from price indicators

When using the co-integration[9] of nominal interest rates to assess convergence levels, Kleimeier and Sander (2000 and 2003) found that the degree of integration was high in corporate lending, moderate in mortgage markets and low in consumer credit markets. Using the harmonised monetary financial institutions (MFI) interest rate statistics for the period from January 2003 to August 2006, Kleimeier and Sander (2007) concluded that mortgage markets[10] exhibited little sign of integration (33% of short-term and 17% of long-term mortgages were co-integrated). Meanwhile, short-term corporate loan markets (with co-integration levels of 75% for small and 100% for large corporate loans) and the market for short-term

---

[6] According to the Eurobarometer Survey (European Commission, 2005e), the majority of EU citizens (85%) have effectively bought a financial product from another member state.

[7] When using the three criteria of the law of one price, cross-border banking business and the market share of foreign banks, Dermine (2006) confirms that there is no strong evidence of market integration in Europe.

[8] More recent evidence on the level of integration in the new EU member states has been more conclusive when observing the high presence of foreign-owned banks in these countries (UniCredit Group, 2008).

[9] Co-integration occurs when lending rates are tied together in a long-term equilibrium relationship that does not demand strict price or product equalisation (c.f. Kleimeier and Sander, 2000, 2003 and 2006; Brada et al., 2005).

[10] This is confirmed by the ECB's report on financial integration in Europe of April 2008 (ECB, 2008).

deposits, time deposits to SMEs and medium-term consumer loans continued to be highly integrated. But owing to the shift from the national retail interest rate (NRIR) to the MFI interest rate, it is not clear to what extent the observed increase in co-integration is truly a sign of more integration or simply reflects the more homogenous nature of the MFI rates over the NRIR rates.

The cross-country dispersion of bank interest rates on loans to households for consumption (Figure 1) purposes has remained relatively high compared with loans to non-financial corporations.[11] In deposit markets, time deposits show the strongest evidence of integration, while demand deposit and savings deposit markets do not appear to be integrated. It should be highlighted that the role of the single currency is central to the analysis, as it has introduced a shift in the structural relationships.

Figure 1. Cross-border standard deviation of MFI interest rates on loans to householders (coefficient of variation)

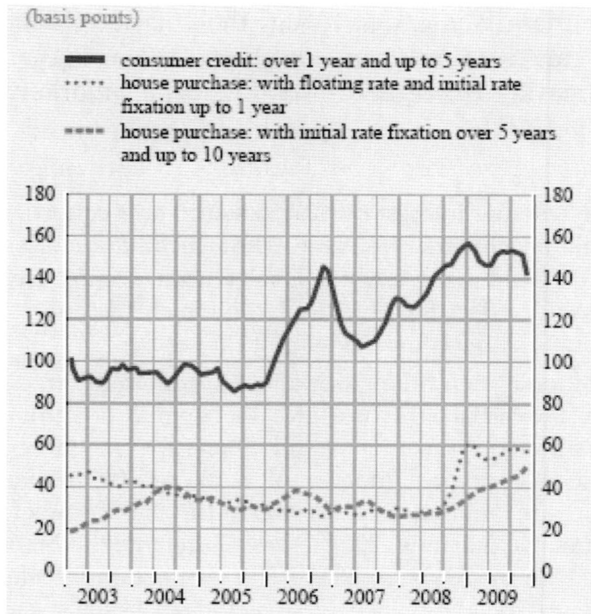

Source: ECB (2010).

---

[11] These differences are mostly explained by the strength in negotiating power of large companies compared with consumers.

When applying the methodology to real interest-rate convergence,[12] country-specific effects have diminished over time, pointing to a reduction in the differences for some selected indicators. Moreover, as shown in Figure 2, the β-coefficient is often negative, indicating that the process of convergence has been continuing over time, although the speed of convergence (given by the size of the coefficient) tends to be far from -1 (complete convergence), and it further decreased as a consequence of the crisis.[13]

Some market participants argue that real interest rate differentials may persist or even increase asymmetries. As underlined by Kleimeier and Sander (2007), regardless of whether Europe attains full convergence of nominal retail loan rates, a country that achieves lower product prices by opening up its market will be punished by higher real interest rates. For this reason, an approach that simultaneously takes product and financial market integration into consideration would be more accurate for assessing price convergence (see also Delgado, 2006).

Other recent evidence[14] based on the pricing structure of retail banking products shows that there was a trend over the course of 2008 towards lower discrepancies across European countries, providing an additional indication of increasing integration in EU retail markets.

---

[12] The idea behind it is to examine whether interest rates across euro area countries have converged towards a specific benchmark over time. The benchmark chosen (σ-convergence) is assumed to be the lowest interest level within a euro area country in each category that should reflect the level towards which the interest rates for the same product in other euro area countries should converge.

[13] Accordingly, factors such as different conditions in national economies (credit and interest rate risk, firm size, industrial structure and the degree of capital market development), institutional factors (taxation, regulation, supervision and consumer protection) and financial structures (degree of bank/capital market financing and competitiveness) are among the barriers to the complete convergence of retail banking. Similarly, Vajanne (2007) assessed the integration of retail banking in the euro area from 2003 to 2006. The estimation of the convergence measures, namely β- and σ-convergence, was used to assess the speed and degree of integration. The tests provided evidence of a process of convergence in retail banks' credit interest rates for households and non-financial corporations and that this convergence is continuing over time.

[14] See the reports by the Consumer Policy Evaluation Consortium (2008) and Capgemini (2008).

Nevertheless, as shown in the next chapter, such an interpretation of the evidence may be over-optimistic.

Figure 2. Beta convergence for selected retail banking interest rates

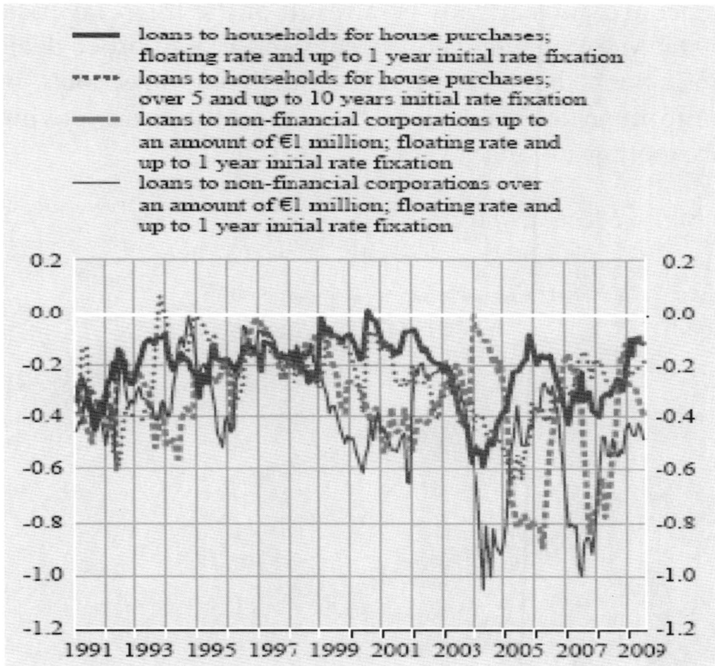

Source: ECB (2010).

Evidence derived from quantity indicators

According to the statistics of the European Central Bank (ECB), the European banking market has undergone a period of consolidation in almost all countries. From 1998 to 2010, the number of credit institutions decreased at an annual average of between 2% and 3% in the eurozone and among the EU-15 countries. This comparable decline was significantly faster before and right after the enlargement with the NMS in 2004, but has levelled out over the past few years. Domestic and cross-border bank mergers (more likely in the EU-15) as well as the entry of foreign banks (in the NMS) can explain this trend. Nonetheless, this situation has been particularly dominated in the number and value of M&As among domestic credit institutions, which represent about 80% of total consolidation activity in the EU over the period 1992–2001.[15] Since 2003, cross-border M&A transactions have displayed slow growth in value, driven by major, scattered acquisitions in the EU-15[16] and a wave of cross-border acquisitions in the NMS. Since 2008, the number and the value of cross-border M&As have declined substantially as a result of the financial crisis (see Figure 3). Domestic M&As have been the rule and cross-border deals the exception. Transactions have been dominated by injections of government capital into financial institutions hit during the crisis, paving the way towards more too-big-to-fail players.

Figure 3. Cross-border banks' M&A activity

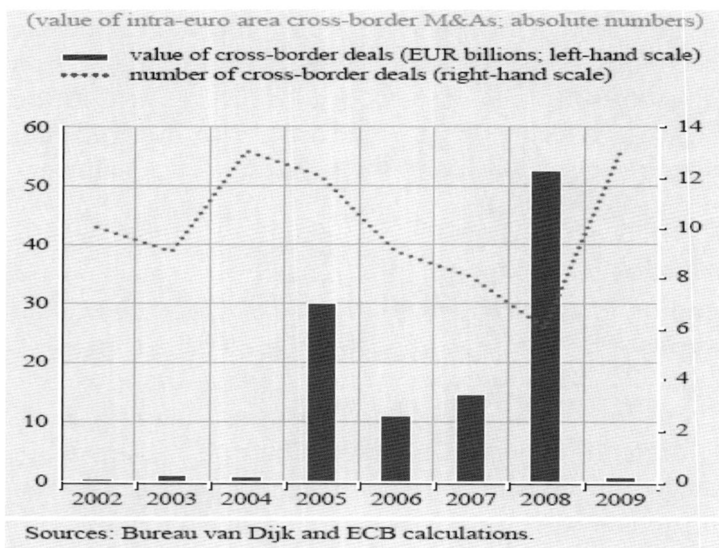

In terms of branch and subsidiary openings, there has been a continued process of gradual market integration. According to CEIOPS (2007), the number of EU/European Economic Area branches increased by around 20% between 2003 and 2005. The median share of assets of branches remained constant at low levels, in contrast to those of subsidiaries, which

---

[15] See Ayadi and Pujals (2004) and European Commission (2005e).

[16] For example, the Dutch ING Bank purchased German and Belgian banks, and the German HypoVerinsbank, after first having acquired Austrian and NMS banks, was subsequently bought by the Italian UniCredito.

have been increasing over the past decade.[17] During the period 2001–06, the average share of foreign establishments of the 'old' EU member states increased from about 25% to nearly 30% in terms of total domestic banking assets, while the respective importance of foreign establishments in the NMS rose from 60% to 70%.[18] The general refocus by EU banks on their domestic market is confirmed by the decline in the market share of other EU branches and subsidiaries in 2008 (18.8% compared with 20.5% in 2007).

In summary, retail financial integration has been an ongoing process over the last decade when assessed through price and quantity-based indicators. Yet since the beginning of the financial crisis and the wave of domestic bailouts, this trend seems to have been broken, with several symptoms – including increased segmentation and a refocus on domestic business – having been observed. The future of financial integration especially in the retail market remains uncertain not only because of the existing obstacles that are inherent to the characteristics of demand and supply of financial services but also as a result of the new challenges brought about by the financial crisis.

Main old and new obstacles to integration

Obstacles to the integration of retail financial services markets are broken down into two categories. The first encompasses the so-called 'natural' barriers, which are mainly demand-driven. These relate to language, cultural preferences[19] and considerations of geographical proximity. Such obstacles are generally difficult to overcome, unless financial players adapt their commercial strategies to consumer preferences and consumers are willing to change their preferences.

The second category of barriers is structural and could be overcome either by market players or by legislative actions. These barriers are mainly related to the high fixed costs incurred in cross-border expansion owing to regulatory, reporting, tax and other impediments.

---

[17] In 2008, subsidiaries remained the preferred form of establishment to access foreign markets, particularly in the EU-12, where EU subsidiaries accounted for around 59% of total assets.

[18] See European Commission (2008b).

[19] According to the ECB's (2008) *Blue Book*, consumers in the UK, for example, seem to have more than two current accounts on average, whereas Italians have fewer than one per citizen.

Consumer-related obstacles

Consumers generally opt for products distributed locally through local institutions, branches, subsidiaries and intermediaries.[20] Indeed, customer mobility is discouraged by information asymmetries and high transaction costs stemming from several factors, such as the fragmentation of market infrastructures (clearing and settlement and payments systems) and legal, consumer protection and tax differences.

Market integration is also likely to be hampered by a lack of consumer awareness of what exists elsewhere,[21] the limited interest in shopping across the board and a lack of confidence. Lack of confidence has been identified especially in the retail market for mortgages, for which consumers may prefer not to change their mortgage contract, may shy away from high switching costs (repayment charges and some administrative costs) and thus remain reluctant to engage in contracts for cross-border financial services.[22] The fact that consumers remain faithful to their existing local providers can also be explained by several shortcomings in European legislation, including the divergences in national civil, commercial, procedural and consumer protection laws. Finally, retail banking tends to remain relationship-based because of the potentially long process of building up a new relationship and in some cases the charges related to closing accounts (up to €60 in Italy) and switching banks.[23]

The lack of confidence has been exacerbated by the lack of protection in the event of the failure of financial institutions. The financial crisis during 2007–09 showed how consumers can incur substantial losses due to the lack or divergence of protection schemes in their country.

---

[20] For more information, see Eurobarometer 230, *Public Opinion in Europe on Financial Services* (European Commission, 2005b).

[21] A recent consumer survey by BME consulting (European Commission, 2007c) showed that on average 36% of the respondents did not know that they could invest their savings in another EU member state (with the lowest proportion (26.4%) found in Germany and the highest (56.5%) in the UK).

[22] According to the European Commission's (2006a) survey, only 3% of respondents indicated that they had considered taking an insurance policy or a mortgage in another member state in the previous 12 months.

[23] Only 7.78% of EU consumers change banks in a given year; see Kleimeier and Sander (2007), pp. v, 3, 31, 54.

Structural and regulatory obstacles

These obstacles have direct consequences on the expansion of supply across countries. Among the structural and regulatory barriers are non-overlapping fixed costs (implying the lack of sufficient cost synergies to offset cross-border M&A costs) and differences in tax treatment,[24] employment legislation and the legal structures of companies. Employees' hostility and local consumers' perceptions also constitute obstacles. Some other barriers relate to divergent supervisory rules and practices, such as multiple reporting requirements and complex processes for supervisory approval, which restrain the potential synergies arising from cross-border consolidation.[25] Finally, legal impediments, nationality discrimination or protectionism inhibit market access and constrain optimal size.

1.3 Integration, efficiency, competition, stability and inclusion

The relationship between integration, efficiency, competition, stability and inclusion is not straightforward. Being integrated is neither a necessary nor a sufficient condition for being a competitive, efficient, stable and inclusive market (see Figure 4).

Figure 4. Conceptual framework of financial integration

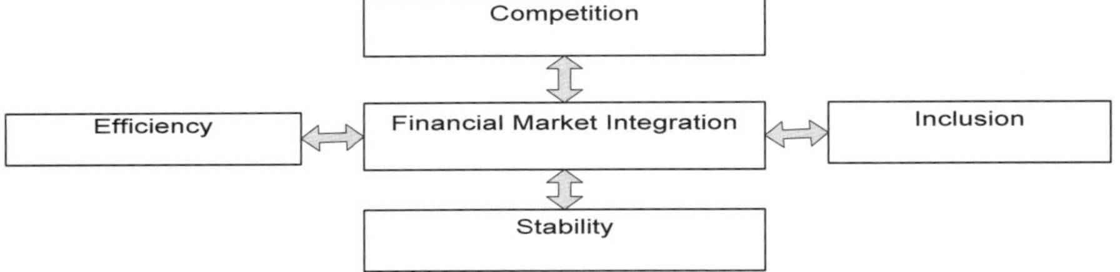

Source: Author's elaboration.

Over the last few years, the EU policy-makers' focus has mainly been on fostering an efficient and competitive, integrated financial market – which is acknowledged as being conducive to more competitiveness and growth. To achieve this objective, regulatory initiatives (the 1999 FSAP) and competition policy measures have complemented each other over time

---

[24] Among them are value added tax (VAT) and other forms of double taxation. See Appendix 2.

[25] See appendix 1 on major obstacles to cross-border consolidation.

despite the limitations related to the enforcement of regulations and the limited scope of analysis of competition policy.

EU policy-makers have nonetheless failed to promote a stable and inclusive integrated market. They have overlooked the need to examine the interactions between competition and stability on the one hand, and efficiency and inclusion on the other. Neither a common framework for financial market stability nor credible inclusive political approaches have been developed to help achieve these two very important pillars in the construction of the internal market for financial services.

In what follows, we examine the interactions between and limitations of the analyses of financial integration, competition, efficiency, stability and inclusion.

Integration and competition

From an institutional perspective, and as discussed in the previous section, more integration can be achieved through the provision of cross-border financial services (through branches, subsidiaries, e-banking, etc.) and consolidation (through M&As, partnerships, alliances, etc.). The theoretical arguments for such a development relate to 'size is beautiful', market power and value creation for shareholders.

Indeed, a more integrated market (through consolidation) does not necessarily mean a more competitive market. In this respect, there is a strong role for competition policy to ensure that in the process of consolidation, financial institutions do not abuse newly formed, dominant positions.

The consolidation wave of the 1990s contributed substantially to changing the market structure of the European financial landscape, especially in the old member states.[26] Concentration has remained asymmetrical, however, because national concentration has significantly increased since 2000 while this has not been the case at the cross-border level. In the last decade, the majority of cross-border transactions have involved financial institutions in the new member states.

Nevertheless, significant differences continue to exist across countries (Figure 5). In some countries, the increase in concentration has reached such proportions that concerns have been voiced about whether it may lead to abuses of market positions. In others, notably in countries where small

---

[26] See Ayadi and Pujals (2004).

and medium-sized banks continue to prevail in the savings or cooperative sectors, there is still room for M&A activity.[27]

Figure 5. Concentration ratio for the top five credit institutions (% of total assets)

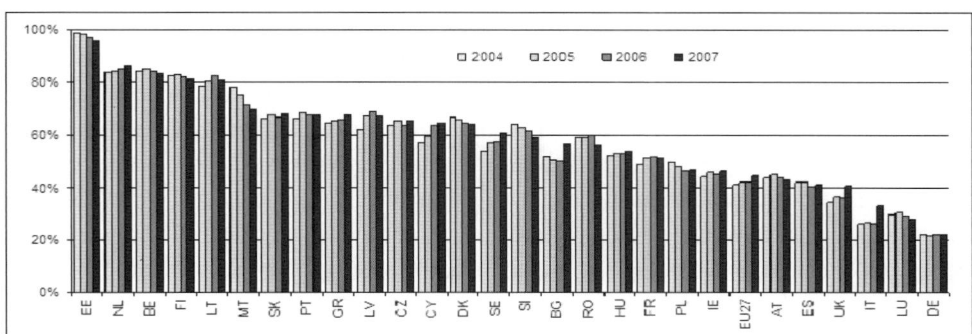

Until recently, there were almost 46 EU banking groups – among a total of 8,000 banks – with significant holdings of cross-border assets and liabilities. These cross-border banks held more than 68% of the total assets of the EU banking sector.[28] Up to three years before the crisis, cross-border M&A activity continued while domestic M&A activity slowed down. Between 2005 and 2007 H1, the annual share of domestic M&As declined to 30% (from 60% between 2000 and 2004) while the annual share of cross-border M&As within the EU increased to 40%[29, 30] (from 20% between 2000

---

[27] Yet measuring the intensity of competition solely with indicators of concentration may be misleading, since these measures apply to an entire national economy, while competition in retail banking takes place in local markets. For example, in the case of Germany, the standard measurements of concentration treat the primary cooperative and savings banks as individual banks. Formally, this is correct, since they are legally independent entities. In an analysis of competition, however, this may be misleading because they also belong to their respective networks and this feature is probably an important competitive strength. If each one of these two groups were treated as one big bank, the concentration figures would be more or less in line with those of other European countries.

[28] Of these banks, 16 groups have been set up by the 'key cross-border players' in the EU: they hold at least 25% of their EU assets outside their home country and were present in at least 25% (i.e. 6) of the other 24 member states. See ECB (2007).

[29] Among the most notable examples in this respect are the merger of the UK-based Abbey National with Banco Santander of Spain in 2005, and the acquisition of the

and 2004). Between 2007 and 2010, further domestic consolidation occurred, particularly in the cooperative sector, while cross-border activity was almost insignificant.

This trend was the result of two complementary stylised facts. On the one hand, domestic bank mergers are limited in some of the Western European markets (e.g. Belgium, Finland or the Netherlands) owing to a high level of market concentration and the high price of acquisitions. On the other hand, because of deregulation and financial liberalisation, emerging Eastern Europe[31] provided the opportunity for exposure to higher growth markets than in many other domestic countries in Western Europe.[32] Exploring these new European markets is explicitly supported by the European Commission, which has revised the European Banking Directive (2006/48/EC) to further promote and foster cross-border bank mergers (see Appendix 1). These tendencies reflect the extent to which concentration in domestic banking systems has reached levels that might impinge on domestic competition and could also cause concerns in terms of anti-competitive behaviour and financial stability in the domestic market (too big to fail, too big for the system and too big to be saved).

It is widely acknowledged that increasing concentration can lead to market power, which may trigger firms to engage in anti-competitive behaviour. Bikker et al. (2006) suggested that the EU banking markets are generally characterised by monopolistic competition, i.e. in which several or many firms offer heterogeneous products and services, thus letting each firm have a certain degree of control over the price of its products and services. Internet banking has played an important and growing role in increasing the contestability of the market. According to the ECB's (2007) report on EU banking structures, in Austria, Germany, Spain, Italy and the UK, online sales of retail banking and especially those by purely Internet banks are progressively more significant. The role of e-banking still faces difficulties, however, ranging from natural barriers (e.g. the preferences

---

Netherlands-based ABN AMRO by a consortium of the UK-based Royal Bank of Scotland, Banco Santander and Belgium-based Fortis Bank in 2007.

[30] A similar trend was observed for the annual share of cross-border M&As in non-EU countries.

[31] This includes the ten new European member states: the Czech Republic, Cyprus, Estonia, Hungary, Latvia, Lithuania, Malta, Poland, Slovakia and Slovenia.

[32] For more details, see *Measuring financial integration in new EU Member States* by Baltzer et al. (2008).

and confidence of consumers, differences in culture or language, and technology) to policy-induced obstacles (e.g. regulation and taxes). From the supplier's perspective, the heterogeneity of payment systems and the problems associated with cross-border clients' identification are also barriers to an integrated e-banking market.

With respect to the resulting effects on consumers' welfare, the evidence remains mixed, with some indications of welfare gains in moderately concentrated banking markets owing to lower lending rates, increased deposit rates and improved credit access.[33]

Consumer behaviour is another structural element that plays an important role. The cross-border mobility of customers is a reflection of more integration and may reduce competitive distortions in the market for financial services. Indeed, a low degree of mobility domestically or across the board would signal the existence of obstacles to switching, which lead to more market power for incumbent banks and barriers to entry for other banks. Furthermore, close cooperation between banks and possible product-tying practices further hinder mobility. Currently, markets such as those for lending and deposits have largely kept their local character through their marketing and distribution. It has been roughly estimated that only 5% of consumers in the EU-15 hold an account in another member state and only 1% use other financial services and this out of necessity in at least three cases (second home, mobile executives and bi-national families), although 26% buy foreign products at home.[34] Moreover, while the retail interest rates among EU member states have declined during the last period, they are still far from converging on an average level.

An investigation by the European Commission, DG Competition (2007b) confirmed the low level of mobility of European customers.[35] The enquiry's results revealed, inter alia, that consumers hold their personal current account with the same bank for around ten years on average, compared with nearly eight years for SMEs in the EU-25 member states.

---

[33] See for instance Walkner and Raes (2005).

[34] For an assessment of the extent of an identified need for simplified, standard financial services products, see European Commission (2004b) and also the report, *The EU market for consumer long-term retail savings vehicles, comparative analysis of products, market structure, costs, distribution systems and consumer saving patterns* (European Commission, 2007c).

[35] Two types of indicators illustrate customer mobility. They are referred to as "churn" and "longevity". See European Commission (2006b).

Behind this overall picture, certain country-level variability persists as those in the EU-15 group of countries engage in longer relationships than those in the NMS,[36] and the longest durations were reported in Nordic countries (Finland, the Netherlands and Sweden).[37] Not surprisingly, these countries were also those that exhibited some of the lowest switching rates, as reported in Table 1. Among the main factors identified as reducing customer mobility in the sector enquiry, cross-selling and the tying of banking products constitute one important channel.[38]

Table 1. Switching rates in the EU-25

Country	Switching rate
Austria	6.57%
Belgium	5.27%
Cyprus	10.33%
Czech Republic	8.61%
Denmark	10.02%
Estonia	k.D
Finland	4.23%
France	6.84%
Germany	8.46%
Greece	2.36%
Hungary	10.41%
Ireland	5.44%
Italy	7.68%
Latvia	6.74%
Lithuania	7.73%
Luxembourg	6.46%
Malta	5.39%
Netherlands	4.17%
Poland	9.11%
Portugal	11.88%
Slovakia	10.81%
Slovenia	5.97%
Spain	12.12%
Sweden	5.62%
United Kingdom	5.07%
EU-25 average	7.78%

Source: European Commission, Report on the retail banking sector inquiry, 31.01.2007

---

[36] The enquiry's estimates of the length of existing current-account relationships report on average 10.40 years (consumers) and 8.56 years (SMEs) for the EU-15 intra-average group against 6.28 years (consumers) and 4.67 years (SMEs) for the EU-10 NMS intra-average group. See European Commission (2007b).

[37] The enquiry's estimates of the length of existing current-account relationships report 17.44 years (consumers) and 13.98 years (SMEs) in Finland, 14.33 years (consumers) and 10.45 years (SMEs) in the Netherlands, 11.82 years (consumers) and 12.33 years (SMEs) in Sweden, and 12.06 years (consumers) and 9.75 years (SMEs) in Denmark. See European Commission (2007b).

[38] See Renda et al. (2009).

Integration and efficiency

Turning to the efficiency effects of integration in the EU, evidence is still highly controversial. Berger et al. (2001) elaborated on the potential for efficiency gains from European integration and related EU policies, such as the single market programme and European monetary union. They hypothesised that international consolidation of financial institutions should be intensified across national boundaries in the EU and should be related to several efficiency effects (i.e. scale, scope and X-efficiency effects). They underlined, however, that the existence of various barriers[39] to cross-border operating efficiency offset most of potential efficiency gains from cross-border consolidation. Casu and Girardone (2007) investigated the integration of EU banking markets by assessing the recent trends in cost efficiency using data envelopment analysis for the EU-15 countries. Their results seem to provide supporting evidence of convergence in efficiency levels towards an EU average.[40] The average, overall efficiency score for the EU banking industry over the entire sample period was 76.5%, indicating a 23.5% average potential reduction in inputs utilisation. Nevertheless, the potential gains brought about by increased integration are offset by a decrease in the overall efficiency levels.

Along the same lines, Ayadi (2006), in analysing M&As in European countries, concluded that there is no evidence of a substantial improvement in cost efficiency for the acquiring bank. In addition, applying the activity/geography matrix, she showed that it is much harder to enhance cost efficiency when the M&A involves different activity profiles. Similarly, her findings show no improvements in profit efficiency for the acquirers or for the targets and that the M&As diversifying geographically intra-EU-15 that were announced up to 2000 failed to improve economic and financial performance.

---

[39] Among them are the difficulty of managing and monitoring institutions from a distant headquarters; differences in language, culture and currency; differences in regulatory/supervisory structures; and differences in explicit or implicit rules against foreign competitors.

[40] Similarly, Weill (2009) investigated the convergence of banking efficiency for European countries between 1994 and 2005. He provided evidence of cross-country improvements in cost efficiency for all EU countries. Alpha and beta convergence tests support the view of a process of convergence in cost efficiency among EU countries.

Hollo and Nagy (2006) concentrated on studying bank efficiency in the enlarged EU. They confirmed the existence of the X-efficiency gap between the banking sectors in the old and new EU member states, but that the competitiveness of the old EU members in relation to cost efficiency was decreasing over time. Kasman and Yildirim (2006) ran a comparative analysis of bank efficiency in eight Central and Eastern European countries. Their results revealed great variability in efficiency and superior efficiency of foreign-owned banks. Therefore, one can expect only limited evidence of the beneficial effects of EU integration and related regulatory and institutional changes for the efficiency of the banking sector in new EU member states.

Integration and stability

With the increasing concentration levels in the national banking markets, institutions have become too big to fail and sometimes too big to save, as shown in Table 2.

Table 2. Too-big-to-fail banks in Europe and the US (top five banks, year-end 2007)

Country	Asset/GDP (%)	Equity/assets (%)
France	293	3.5
Germany	165	2.6
Italy	131	7.4
Iceland	890	6.3
Ireland	404	3.6
Luxembourg	854	5.2
Netherlands	521	3.8
Spain	184	7.2
Switzerland	756	3.2
UK	313	3.9
US	44	7.6

Source: Bankscope Database.

The large size of these banks poses a serious concern for their domestic market and also for other markets where they are established through a branch or a subsidiary. A disastrous impact was shown when the top Icelandic banks (which accounted for more than 800% of Iceland's

GDP) were bailed out by the state, nearly resulting in sovereign bankruptcy. In a crisis situation and in the absence of a credible European framework for financial stability, uncertainties are likely to reinforce market disarray. The events during the 2007–09 crisis gave a vivid illustration of the weaknesses in the construction of the internal market for financial services.

From a retail perspective, depositors in a panic made a run on a previously reputable UK bank, Northern Rock, notwithstanding the UK deposit insurance system; furious investors lost years of savings in one of the leading Belgian banks, Fortis, and in subsidiaries of Icelandic banks.

Moreover, the degree to which banks might be at risk from market turbulence, as can be measured by the capitalisation ratio (capital as a percentage of total assets), which is supposed to assess their solidity, also varies considerably from one member state to another. German banks appear to be the least capitalised in Europe, holding core capital of 2.6% meaning €2.6 in capital for every €100 of assets. By contrast, Italian banks hold about three times as much capital (€7.4 per €100 of total assets). In an integrated market, such discrepancies are hardly sustainable.

In addition, the protection of such institutions raises important competitive issues and can generate moral hazard incentives in the long run. This reveals a poorly explored relationship between stability, competition and integration, which until today, has been overlooked by policy-makers. In addition, rules that typically apply can be waived or ignored or leniently interpreted (e.g. state aid rules in the EU or fiscal rules for the eurozone member states) in a crisis context.

Integration and inclusion

While financial institutions are racing to increase capitalisation and profits through the strategies they opt for (for example, cross-border M&As), financial exclusion emerges as a critical issue and deserves careful independent assessment. The apparent dichotomy between a 'free competition' model and the 'public good' aspect of basic financial services is at the heart of the policy debate on tackling financial exclusion and ultimately social exclusion.

Financial exclusion appears to be a growing problem in the EU.[41] Within a context of market liberalisation, increased competition, integration and technological development, "the general economic interest missions are means by which a balance may be struck between competition and protecting more vulnerable consumers".[42] Hence, the financial services industry has an important role in ensuring the access to and use of basic financial services by every citizen. Obviously, this role depends on the country in question[43] and the interaction of several factors, including the market structure, the financial institutions' business models, the dual bottom line nature of the institutions and the role of the government at the national and regional levels. Clearly, there is a need to consider the possible friction between the race for more integration, notably through national and cross-border champions, more economic efficiency and social cohesion, which could be enhanced by a diverse banking sector serving a multitude of market segments.[44] Indeed, many financial institutions (particularly shareholder value institutions) face imperatives of value creation, shareholders' satisfaction and expansion of activities beyond national borders. This pressure not only requires them to opt for programmes of cost reductions (including branch closures in remote areas) but may also result in poor incentives to supply unprofitable basic financial services and so forth. These impulses are contradictory to enhancing financial inclusion and social cohesion.

In conclusion, to ensure a balanced interaction between integration, efficiency, competition, stability and inclusion, and in line with the European 2020 smart, sustainable and inclusive growth strategy, the European Commission must revisit the philosophy for the internal market for financial services, with a view towards a more balanced approach and one that is aligned with the new European growth strategy. A post-crisis Financial Services Action Plan must be drafted, while factoring in equally these four concepts that are crucial to the future of financial market integration.

---

[41] According to Eurostat (2006), around 16% of the EU population lives on less than 60% of the median national income, the low-income threshold set to measure relative poverty.

[42] See Carbó et al. (2005).

[43] See Ayadi and Rokiewitcz (2008).

[44] See Ayadi et al. (2009 and 2010).

2. MARKETS AND POLICY ASSESSMENT

In this chapter, we assess market and policy initiatives to foster integration in retail financial services. The chapter covers payments, credit and investment markets.

2.1 Payments market

The popularity of payment instruments varies across the EU. The most predominant forms of these transactions (in terms of total value) are credit transfers and direct debits (both of which are Single European Payments Area (SEPA) instruments). Although they are frequently conducted (see Figure 6, panel a), point-of-sale (POS) payments[45] comprise less than 10% of GDP, except in a handful of countries (Figure 6, panel b). The use of cheques as a means of payment is still prevalent in a number of highly ranked countries, such as Cyprus, France, Ireland, Malta, Portugal and the UK.

Figure 6. Payment instruments in Europe in 2007

Panel a

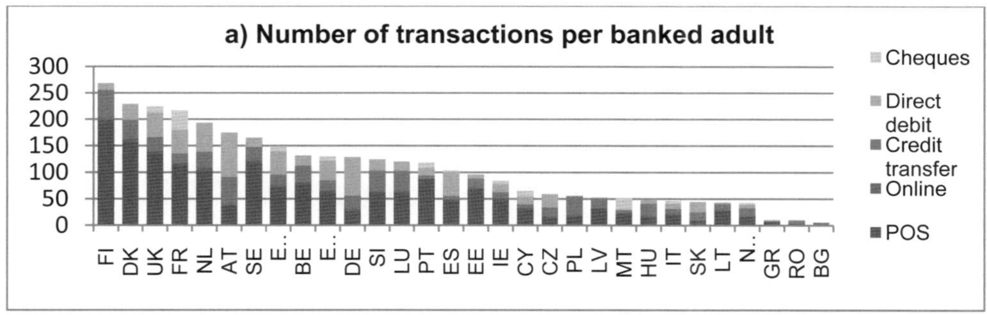

---

[45] These are payment transactions initiated through a POS terminal using a card with debit, credit or delayed-debit functions.

Panel b

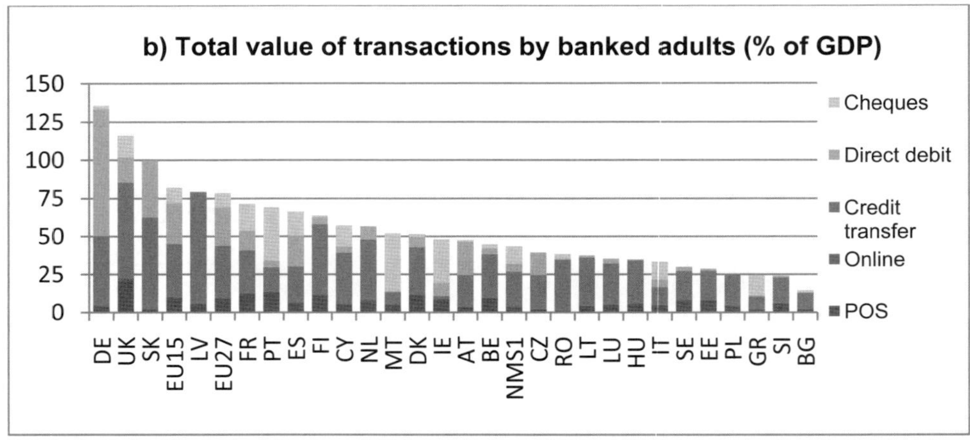

Source: ECB *Blue Book* (2008).

As illustrated in Figure 7, there is a high degree of diversity in the tariffs for payment instruments among countries in the EU. The prevalence of such discrepancies makes cross-border price comparability difficult to achieve.

Figure 7. Pricing of payment instruments (€)

a) Pricing of credit transfers

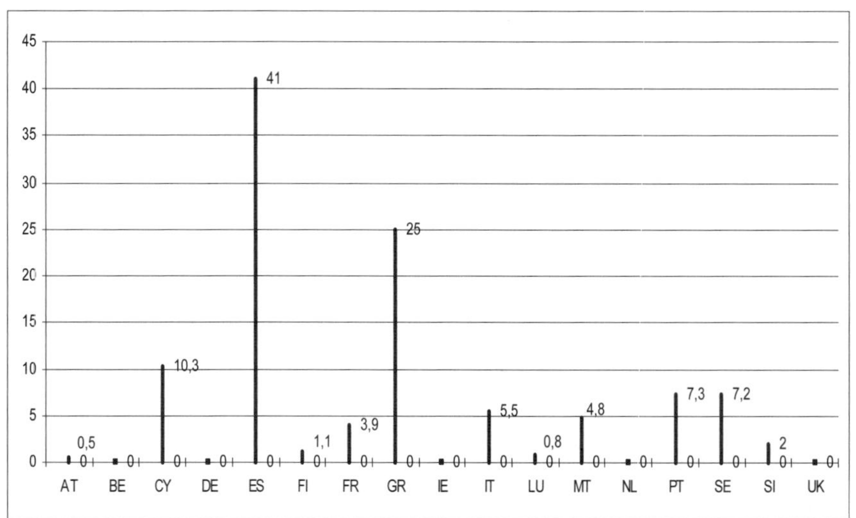

b) Pricing of direct debit

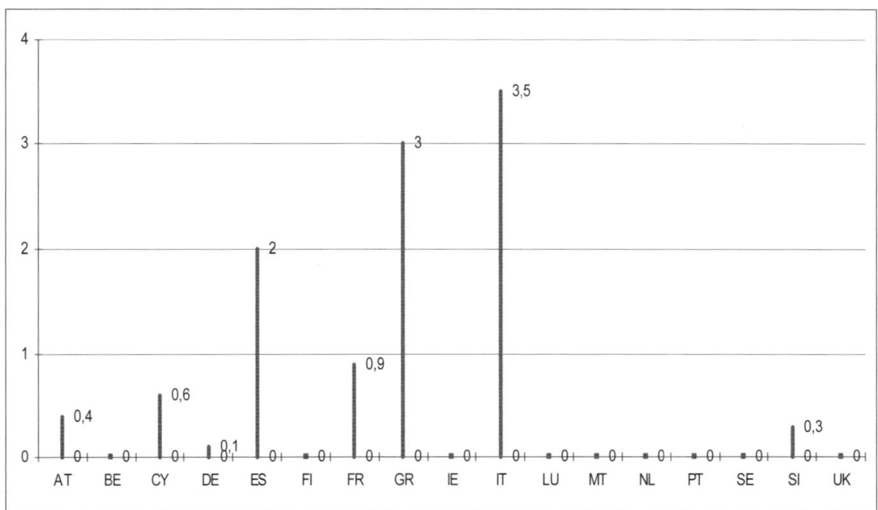

c) Pricing of debit cards

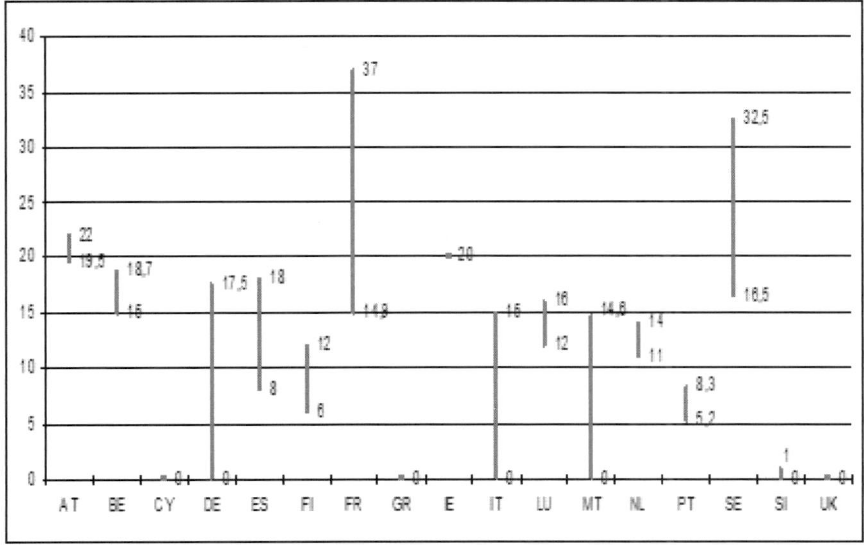

d) Pricing of delayed debit and credit cards

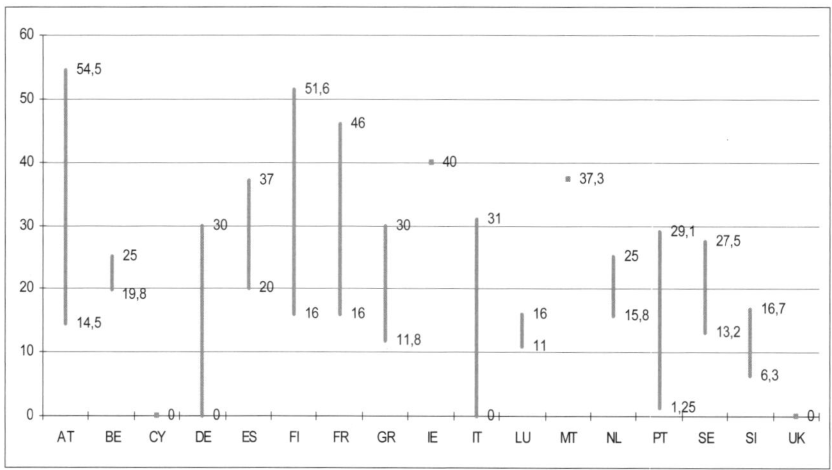

Source: European Commission (2008a).

As far as current accounts[46] are concerned, there is wide diversity in pricing across the 27 member states. In a profile on average usage, Italy, Spain and France rank at the top while the new EU member states rank at the bottom.[47] This discrepancy is a result of different competitive conditions, cost structures, pricing models, and the level of tying and bundling of products. The breakdown of annual charges[48] shows that the

---

[46] These accounts typically include all payment instrument plus opening and closing charges.

[47] This ranking does not take the purchasing power parity (PPP) into account; yet when applying PPP, the ranking does not change.

[48] The breakdown covers the following annual charges:

- *basic annual charges*, including package fees and account maintenance charges;
- *account charges*, including charges for opening and closing an account, statements, overdrafts and insufficient funds, over-the-counter withdrawals and deposits, account movements, Internet and phone banking, and income related to credit interest on accounts in credit;
- *debit card charges*, including issuance and annual fees, fees for blocking and replacement, and charges for withdrawals, POS and online payments;
- *credit card charges*, including issuance and annual fees, fees for blocking and replacement, and charges for withdrawals, POS and online payments;

persistence of this discrepancy across the 27 EU member states (see Figure 8, panels a and b).

Figure 8. Pricing of current accounts in Europe (in 2009)

Panel a

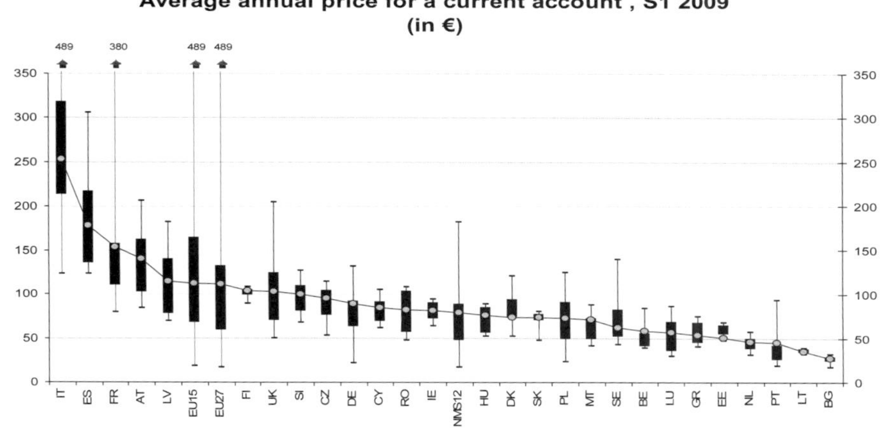

Panel b

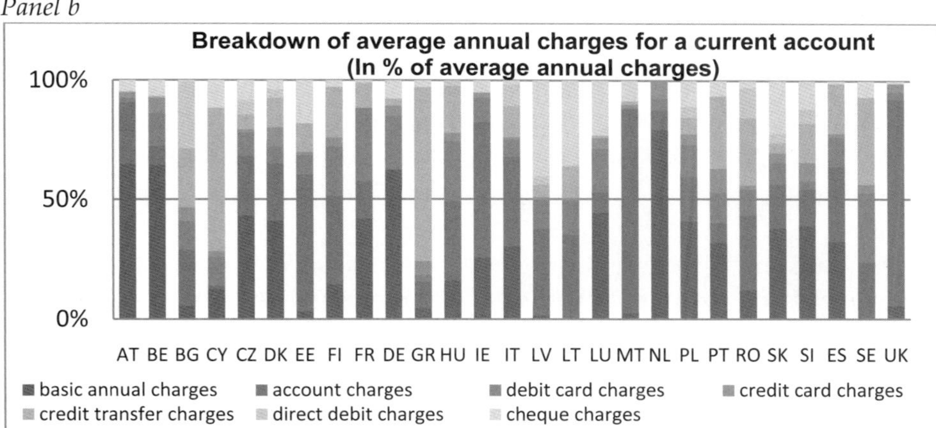

Source: European Commission (2009d).

- *credit transfer charges*, including fees for receiving and sending credit transfers, receiving and sending standing orders and charges for setup, modification and closure of standing orders;
- *direct debit charges*, including fees for sending direct debits, and the setup and closure of direct debit orders; and
- *cheque-related charges*, including fees for the order of chequebooks, along with drawing, lodging and bouncing cheques.

It is expected that SEPA[49] will lead to more harmonisation in the tariffs for payment instruments[50] across EU member states. Several potential (not yet proven), positive changes are sought for consumers, merchants and the industry (see Table 3). These changes will not be without costs for the end-users, however.

Table 3. SEPA's potential impacts on end-users

Users	SEPA's potential impacts
Consumers	• More universal and predictable payments and transfers from/to home banks to/from any other SEPA country using common standards
	• More choice of products and services at more competitive prices
	• Wider choice of purchases and cash withdrawals across SEPA countries
	• Improvements in the safety and security of purchases and cash withdrawals
	• Full transparency and disclosure of charges, fees and exchange rates
	• Common legal framework for refunds, disputes and complaints

---

[49] SEPA is defined in the European Payments Council (EPC) Roadmap in December 2004 as "the area where citizens, companies and other economic actors will be able to make payments in euro within Europe whether between or within national boundaries under the same basic conditions, rights and obligations, regardless of their locations" (see the EPC website, "What is SEPA?", http://www.europeanpaymentscouncil.eu/content.cfm?page=sepa_vision_and_goals).

The main aim of SEPA is to improve the efficiency of the cross-border euro retail payments and to restructure and modernise fragmented national payment instruments with the implementation of new, common business rules and technical standards. The legal underpinning of SEPA is the Payment Services Directive, which has been transposed into national laws since November 2009. The Payment Services Directive covers the right to provide payment services to the public by all payment services providers; the transparency and information requirements to protect consumers; and rights and obligations of users and providers of payment services. On 28 January 2008, SEPA was officially launched by the European Commission, the ECB and the European Payments Council. Since then, the first SEPA credit transfer and direct debit payments have been made possible through the plans of all market participants to progressive migrate to the new SEPA payment products (by end 2010).

[50] SEPA payment instruments – credit transfers, direct debits and card payments – are to migrate to interoperable formats and processes across all of the euro area and future SEPA participants.

Table 3. cont'd

Merchants	• The ability to accept payments from all SEPA countries leading to more sale possibilities • Reduced cash holding and improved security • Reduction of fraud in card payments and a harmonised framework for fraud management and reporting • Terminal and transaction cost reductions through economies of scale • Simplified back office processes (also for banks) • Wider choice for acquirer services
Large merchants and corporates (additional)	• Construction of a standard platform for their euro payment operations because of common standards • Fewer barriers to expansion stemming from payment processing constraints and the reduction of commercial and technical barriers • Major savings from 1) exemption processing, 2) automated standing data setup, and 3) better and guaranteed remittance data
SMEs (additional)	• Improved cash flows and the reduction of processing costs owing to faster settlements and simplified processing • New, consistent legal framework for payments and redress to boost cross-border selling • More euro payments possible with more certainty and clarity • More efficient transfers for purchases and greater choice of payment products
Government and public adminis-trators	• Common schemes operating to common standards are expected to deliver better services to citizens • Procurement of payment services will no longer be limited to local banks • Simpler regulatory monitoring of providers of payment services
Banks	• Supply of accounts that are usable in all SEPA countries, regardless of size • Development of innovative products at a lower cost through technology and homogeneous standards • New market opportunities (access to business with large merchants and corporates, M&A possibilities from the reduction of country-specific platform costs, new value-added services) • More options for the procurement process • More transparency and clarity of charges • Reduction of internal and external costs

Source: Author's compilation.

In theory, retail consumers should be able to pay with their debit cards everywhere in Europe, to use the same bank accounts even when studying and working abroad and to use direct debits from anywhere in Europe. Yet these expectations depend on the costs, pricing and quality standards of the new SEPA instruments, the information consumers receive, the service quality in terms of helping consumers to use the IBAN and BIC codes, and solving issues pertaining to the security of direct debits and whether consumer mobility is facilitated and competition fostered.

According to a study by AT Kearney,[51] banks are expected to make significant investments in payment systems at both the front and back ends. Costs will be even greater, particularly in the absence of a phase-out date for national instruments, during the coexistence of old and new instruments for an undetermined length of time and the uncertainty surrounding the 'voluntary' process for migration. Such costs will be passed on to end-users of payment instruments.

As shown above, end-users face vastly different pricing structures for similar instruments. For example, a debit card transaction in Denmark is free to the merchant, while in other countries merchants are charged a service fee of up to 1.5%. In most countries, debit cards are either free or carry a low annual fee (from €5 to €10), while in France the annual fee is between €30 and €40. SEPA is expected to foster competition while alleviating many of these differences as banks and payment providers seek to find a fair pricing structure for their products across Europe. SEPA instruments will not come without a cost and the low price of domestic instruments might not always be sustainable in light of the new instruments. Several services – including encryption, fraud detection and other sophisticated standards – are costly and therefore selective price increases might be required, especially for cards. Operating a pan-European infrastructure cannot be without a certain transactional fee. As a consequence, there is an expectation that low-fee countries, such as Denmark, the Netherlands and Belgium, might face price increases, while other countries like France might see price decreases for payment and card users. The average effect will likely be a price reduction but not necessarily an aggressive race to the bottom. There is also an expectation towards convergence on a fair pricing structure, albeit with uncertainty with respect to the determination of the fair price and the sharing mechanism among

---

[51] See the AT Kearney (2008) study on *The SEPA shake-out: Challenges in cards and payments*.

providers. A provider that dominates a certain market will be less price-sensitive and therefore will be advantaged.

With the integration of the markets, smaller players will find it difficult to bear the new investments, which come at a fixed cost and may not be offset by a large number of transactions. Only a limited number of international and pan-European players will be able to leverage their European networks and volumes to amortise these investments, particularly when it comes to value added services (such as guaranteed payments and advanced reporting facilities). The good news is that SEPA will allow payment providers in general to expand more easily across Europe as instruments become similar and traditional country barriers are removed. This is already happening in a number of places for both payments and cards (e.g. the merger between Interpay Nederland and the German company Transaktionsinstitut to form Equens, a pan-European provider that is becoming active in Belgium, Finland, Italy and other countries). The expectation is that large providers will emerge in the European landscape and pursue international growth opportunities. In the longer term, they may be able to offer a significantly lower price point, but that is not certain. The challenge for all providers in the short term is to integrate their legacy systems in different countries and operate on one scale curve across countries as opposed to operating separate platforms with separate scale curves in each market.

Non-bank payment providers (telecom operators, for example) are expanding in emerging segments (payments for music and movie downloads through mobile invoices). As customers become accustomed to the convenience of such payments, the mobile operator can charge a higher commission on each transaction. Banks are beginning to respond to this threat, leading to an increasingly competitive market in the future, notably with radio frequency identification technology becoming ubiquitous and the growing importance of the e-payments space (PayPal[52] and Google Checkout have both applied for a banking licence in Europe and since mid-2007 they have had a European passport). Another area of non-bank competition is money transfer services. Companies like MoneyGram, Western Union and Travelex are best positioned to expand their business among immigrants and low-income consumer groups.

---

[52] Already, PayPal has 153 million user accounts (of which more than 35 million are in Europe).

Until recently, the migration to new SEPA instruments (i.e. credit transfers) has been below expectations. Only 9.3% of the total credit transfers in Europe used a SEPA transfer in August 2010. These numbers mask substantial country-specific differences, with levels in Luxembourg (89.9%) and Cyprus (56.6%) at end-2009 well above the percentage considered the critical mass (around 50%), while migration in Germany or Ireland was marginal.

For direct debit payments, it is still premature to make a comprehensive assessment. In August 2010, only 0.07% of all executed direct debit transactions were processed in the SEPA format. This is due to the fact that the launch of the SEPA direct debit scheme took place almost two years after the introduction of SEPA credit transfers and banks have only gradually been offering these new services. As of 1 November 2010, however, banks have been *required* by Regulation (EC) No. 924/2009[53] to be reachable for cross-border direct debits.

The hesitation to migrate to SEPA is partly related to the impacts of the financial crisis on the financial industry, merchants and public authorities, all of which are reluctant to make the necessary investments to support the migration process.

All in all, owing to the diverse payment systems, payment habits, payment providers' cost structures and levels of cost efficiencies and pricing in the member states, it is important to ensure a systematic monitoring of the changes (volume and pricing) of the new SEPA instruments, not only for the banking and payment industry but also for the end-users of these instruments.

2.2 Credit market

The financial crisis has significantly impacted the previously robust growth of European retail credit markets.[54]

---

[53] Regulation (EC) No. 924/2009 of the European Parliament and of the Council of 16 September 2009 on cross-border payments in the Community and repealing Regulation (EC) No. 2560/2001, OJ L 266, 9.10.2009.

[54] Retail credit encompasses all lending to the household sector (including non-profit institutions serving households) and includes 'consumer credit', 'loans for house purchases' and 'other lending'. According to definitions of the European Central Bank, *consumer credit* is "loans granted to households for personal use in the consumption of goods and services". A *loan for a house purchase* is "credit extended to households for the purpose of investment in housing, including

Figure 9 shows that in more than three-quarters of the EU member states, the loans granted to households in 2008 grew at a slower pace than in 2007, when the then-looming credit crunch started to drag on real annual growth rates.

These aggregate numbers, however, hide major country-specific differences among EU member states: while the Eastern European countries experienced the fastest relative growth with double-digit figures of real increases despite the unfavourable macroeconomic conditions caused by the crisis, the more mature (Western European) markets witnessed rather moderate (or even negative) real growth.

Figure 9. Real annual growth rates of total credit to households in the EU-27 member states

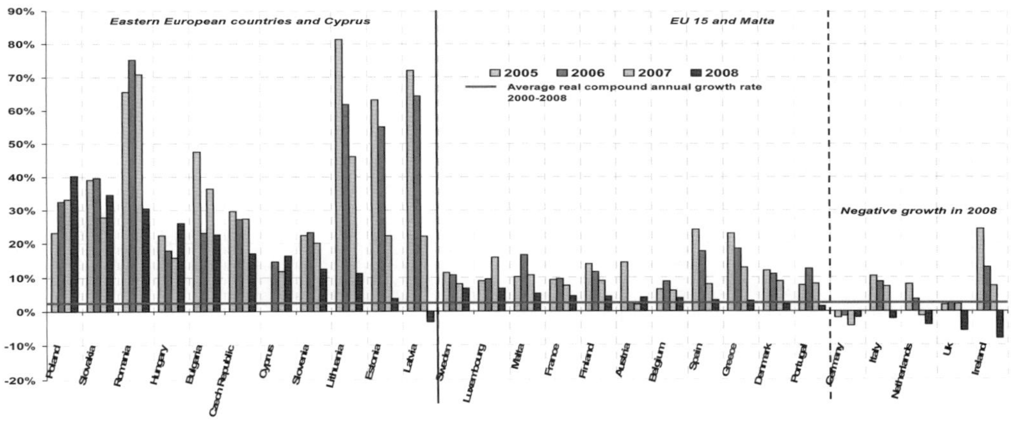

Source: ECRI (2009).

Similar variations among European markets become evident when looking at the credit-to-GDP ratio (Figure 10). On an aggregate level, the growth of credit granted to European households has been outpacing the

---

building and home improvements, [also covering] loans secured by residential property (i.e. mortgage loans) that are used for house purchase and, where identifiable, other loans for house purchase provided on a personal basis or secured by other types of asset[s]". *Other lending* constitutes the residuum volume of "credit other than consumer credit and loans for house purchase that is extended to households for special purposes such as business needs, the procurement of office equipment, debt consolidation, education, the purchase of securities, etc." (see the ECB's website, "Glossary", http://www.ecb.int/home/glossary/html/index.en.html).

increase in GDP since 2000, causing a steady rise in the weighted, average relative indebtedness of European households. The ratio is currently 20% higher than ten years ago, having peaked at 64.44% the year before the crisis hit in 2007. But in 2008, the total credit to households as a percentage of GDP for the EU-27 contracted for the first time since 1998, declining 150 basis points to 62.9%, a drop following a yearly average increase of 1.5 percentage points over the previous ten years.

Figure 10. Total credit to households in the EU-27 (% of GDP)

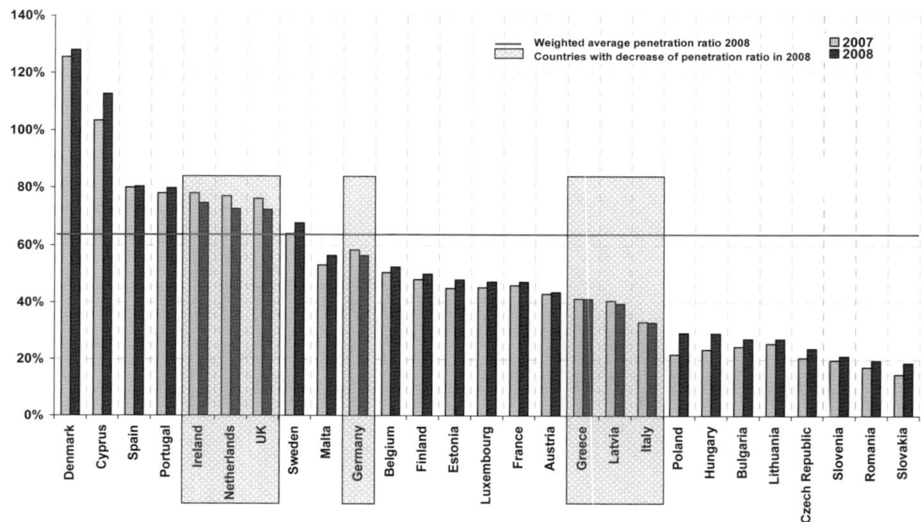

Source: ECRI (2009).

A closer look of the aggregate retail credit market in Europe shows that on average, loans for house purchases account for more than two-thirds of the credit portfolio of European households. This is the case despite the end of an upward trend in 2008 in the share of housing loans, which peaked at 69.1% in 2007, after a 12% increase since 2001. The remaining third is split between consumer credit and other loans, the latter of which – among other things – are being used for debt consolidation. While all three segments of household credit contracted in the course of the worsening financial turmoil in the years 2007–08, growth rates dropped significantly in the area of loans for house purchases and consumer credit. Figure 11 illustrates this development and reflects that both segments even experienced negative growth in 2008.

Figure 11. Year-on-year growth of loans for house purchases and consumer credit in the EU

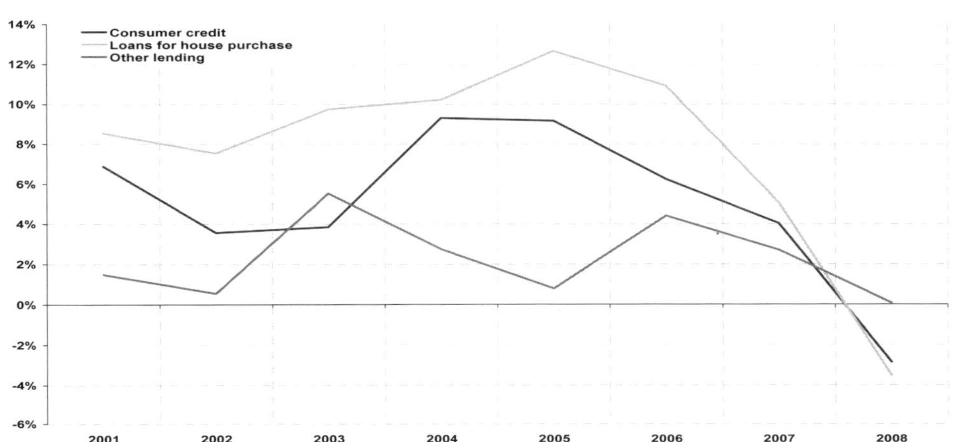

Source: ECRI (2009).

In the absence of a commonly accepted set of tools for the measurement of (retail credit) market integration, the considerably varying figures depicting current credit market realities (credit-to-GDP ratio, inflation-adjusted market growth rates, consumption financed by loans, the relative weight of loans for house purchases vs. consumer credit, etc.) within the EU can serve as a rough indicator for the level of credit market integration. Quantity-based indicators, such as the shares of cross-border loans extended by monetary financial institutions (MFIs) to non-banks as a percentage of total euro area provision of financial services, draw a similarly bleak picture: the numbers have barely risen from 3.1% in 1999 to only 5.7% as of end-2008.[55]

Often, similar reactions to external shocks such as the drops in real annual growth rates across the majority of member states in the wake of the financial crisis are referred to in order to underline ongoing tendencies in retail credit market integration. In particular, analogous movements of national interest rates owing to certain shocks have been referred to frequently as the best way to measure integration – despite certain

---

[55] Data are provided by the ECB and represent aggregate figures of lending to the non-bank private sector. Data on cross-border lending to households alone are not available.

shortcomings.[56] But a look at the most recent data (Figure 12) illustrates strong dispersion in both the consumer credit and housing loan markets during the financial crisis with no signs of a declining trend in the near future.

Figure 12. Cross-country standard deviation of MFI interest rates on loans to households (basis points)

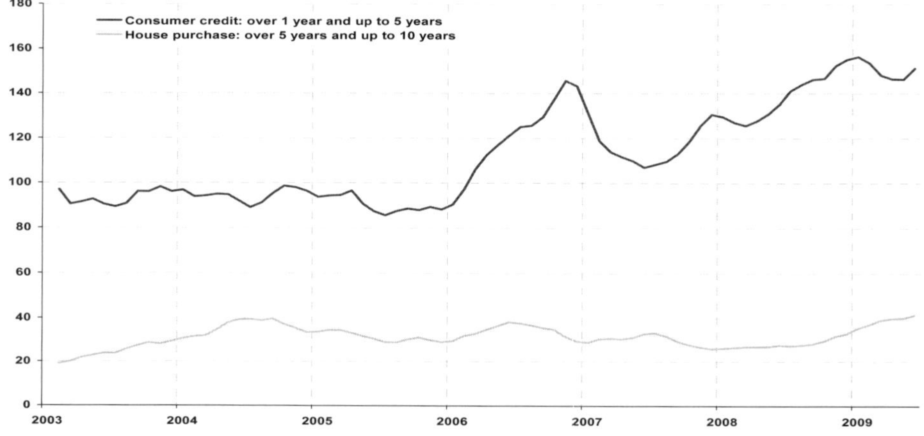

Source: ECB, Indicators of financial integration in the euro area.

Retail credit markets have become more competitive over the last two decades – leading to increased choice and a broader range of (innovative) products available to a wider population for (on average) lower prices – but EU markets remain fragmented despite various attempts to quantify the potential benefits of a single market for credit. A study on the costs and benefits of the integration of EU mortgage markets,[57] for example, estimates a rise of EU GDP by 0.7% and private consumption by 0.5% over a period of ten years (2005–15). Another study by Mercer Oliver Wyman and the

---

[56] A pure analysis of price data may neglect variations in underlying credit risks or differences in product design, supplier efficiencies, goals for returns on investment, tax regimes, early repayment options and the general regulatory framework, etc.

[57] See the report on *The Costs and Benefits of Integration of EU Mortgage Markets* (European Commission, 2005c).

European Mortgage Federation estimates the benefits of EU mortgage market integration in the area of 0.12-0.24% of EU GDP per annum.[58]

Notwithstanding these figures nor the predominant position of housing loans in the credit portfolio of European households, mortgage lending is currently not yet regulated at the European level. Concrete legislative action has so far only been taken in the area of consumer credit, when in May 2008 the new Consumer Credit Directive (2008/48/EC)[59] was adopted, aimed at achieving a higher level of consumer protection, enhancing responsible lending practices and harmonising the definition of the annual percentage rate (APR) of charge. To enhance the comparability of different offers, the directive foresees the provision of clear, understandable and comprehensive pre-contractual (and contractual) information in a standardised form (Standard European Consumer Credit Information).

As regards mortgage lending, on the other hand, the Commission has been relying on a voluntary code of conduct since its inception in September 2002 as an appropriate means to supply information on housing loans and to encourage cross-border competition. According to the *Third Progress Report on Implementation in the EU* (EBIC, 2009), the code is adhered to in 20 member states (plus Norway), with coverage of between 90% and 100% in 14 member states.

The lack of concrete (proposals for further) regulation, however, should not be seen as mere inactivity on the part of the European Commission services in the area of retail credit. Ever since the adoption of the *White Paper on the Integration of EU Mortgage Credit Markets* (European Commission, 2007g), the Commission has been engaging in a variety of evaluations and stakeholder interactions, aimed at assessing the costs and benefits of further regulatory measures (see appendix 3). In late 2008, the Commission called upon a group of experts to come forward with concrete recommendations for doing away with existing barriers to the single market in the area of collecting and sharing credit data. Existing obstacles to cross-border access to borrowers' credit data are seen to effectively hinder the cross-border provision of credit. The 2009 report by the Expert

---

[58] See the *Study on the Financial Integration of European Mortgage Markets* by Mercer Oliver Wyman and the European Mortgage Federation (2003).

[59] Refer to Directive 2008/48/EC of the European Parliament and of the Council of 23 April 2008 on credit agreements for consumers and repealing Council Directive 87/102/EEC, OJ L 133/66, 22.5.2008.

Group on Credit Histories,[60] having regard to privacy and other consumer protection concerns on the one side and the potential disproportional nature of costs and benefits on the other, rejected the option of creating a pan-European credit register or aligning all member states with an existing or newly established mechanism for sharing credit data. So far, no decision has been taken concerning the transposition of the Expert Group's recommendations into guidelines or their implementation through further regulation. Additionally, a study by the European Commission on credit intermediaries in the internal market[61] shed light on current market realities, the specific forms of potential consumer detriment as well as possible regulatory responses to structural market inefficiencies. With the latest public consultation on responsible lending and borrowing[62] seeking advice and comments on options for registration and supervision of credit intermediaries, the Commission is currently evaluating the costs and benefits of future intervention in an until-now (on the EU level) practically unregulated market.

The present political uncertainty surrounding the next steps in developing the European retail credit market is aggravated by the broad nature of the ambitious responsible lending and borrowing agenda of the European Commission.[63] The latter ranges from questions concerning pre-contractual information, product standardisation/certification, the facilitation of creditworthiness checks and the (mandatory?) introduction of supplementary suitability checks to issues regarding marketing, advertising and financial advice as well as the previously mentioned operation of credit intermediaries. As re-opening the Consumer Credit Directive dossier is deemed politically too difficult (with transposition still underway, having exceeded the June 2010 deadline), the question arises of how to best introduce legislative measures, if necessary, in the (non-)existing framework.

---

[60] See European Commission (2009b).

[61] See the *Study on Credit Intermediaries in the Internal Market* (European Commission, 2009c).

[62] For further information, see the European Commission's Internal Market website, "Responsible lending and borrowing", "Consultation on Responsible Lending and Borrowing the EU" (2009) (http://ec.europa.eu/internal_market/finservices-retail/credit/responsible_lending_en.htm#consultation).

[63] Derived from the recommendations in the CEPS/ECRI (2011) Task Force report, *A new retail credit regime for Europe: Setting the right priorities* (forthcoming).

2.3 Retail investment market

The retail investment fund industry in Europe grew steadily until 2007 to reach the level of €7,909 billion. The year 2008 marked a break in the trend due to the financial crisis and the unfortunate events in the financial markets (the demise of Lehman Brothers and the scandal linked to Madoff funds, in which major European fund managers had invested) (see Figure 13). The growth of this market cannot ignore the inherent market failings, which include the asymmetries of information that exist between investors and the industry/sellers and the intrinsic conflict-of-interest problem when designing and distributing these products.

Figure 13. Net assets of European investment funds (€ billions)

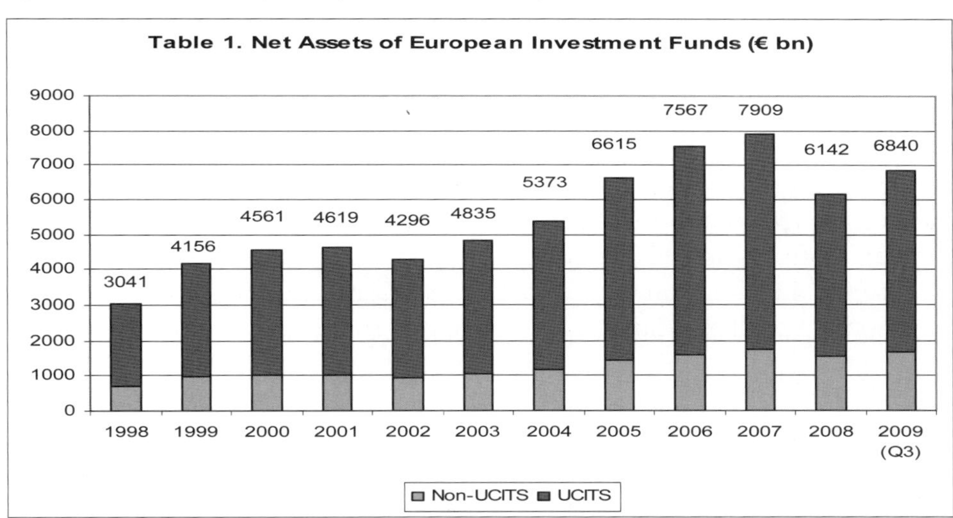

Source: Efama (2009).

The EU passport has certainly facilitated the quantity of cross-border sales, a chief indicator for assessing market integration. For example, the number of foreign funds accessible domestically was larger than the number of domestic funds in the majority of the EU-15 countries in 2005 (see Figure 14). Still, the quality of this varied supply left much to desire.

Figure 14. Number of funds available in national markets (31 December 2005)

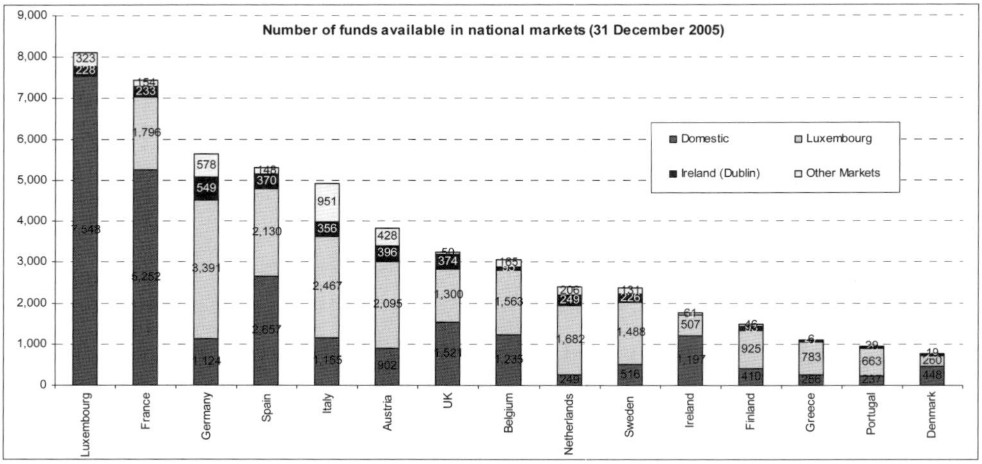

Source: ZEW (2006).

EU regulation governing the free provision of financial services in the asset management industry across borders under home country rules started with the UCITS Directive of 1985 (85/611/EEC). The UCITS Directive introduced harmonised *product* regulation for investment funds that were allowed for cross-border sales in the EU (and the countries of the European Economic Area). It was followed in the early 1990s with directives defining the terms under which the banking, insurance and investment services sectors could 'passport' their *services* across the EU on the basis of authorisation from their home state regulator. The UCITS Directive was amended and expanded in 2002 and later in 2009, to become more of a horizontal asset-management directive to reflect the increasing convergence of the core sectors of the financial services industry. An agreement was also reached in 2002 on the last outstanding piece of regulation on the free provision of cross-border services in the financial services sector, the Pension Funds Directive (2003/41/EC). In the meantime, the new wave of the FSAP had started to come into effect, most importantly with the MiFID (Markets in Financial Instruments Directive, 2006/48/EC).

The 1985 UCITS Directive paved the way for the cross-border sale of investment funds in the EU. Subject to some general criteria regarding authorisation, legal structure, investment policies and disclosure, units of open-ended funds that invest in transferable securities could be sold freely throughout the EU. The 2002 UCITS amendments expanded the scope of activities that were possible under the UCITS I Directive. One directive –

the UCITS III Product Directive – widens the investment possibilities of funds to include instruments like derivatives and allows for new forms of funds, such as funds of funds, money market funds, cash funds or index tracker funds. A second directive – the UCITS III Management Directive – detailed minimum standards, including the introduction of a minimum level of own funds to be held by a fund management company for prudential purposes, and broadened the permissible activities of the fund management company. It also introduced a simplified prospectus, which provides for key factual information about a UCITS to be presented to investors in an accessible and uniform format. The UCITS III Directive grants the 'single license' to fund management companies in the broad sense of the word. It comprises not only the management of investment funds – i.e. the core services – but also other activities related to portfolio management, such as pension funds for individuals, investment advice, safekeeping (custody) and administration of investment funds, which are seen as non-core or ancillary.[64]

In 2007, the European Commission proposed a further set of amendments to the directive. UCITS IV was formally adopted by the EU in April 2009, and it is expected to be implemented by July 2011 at the latest. The latest amendments formally allow for a genuine European passport for UCITS management companies, enabling the separation between the location of the management company from the place where funds are registered. UCITS IV facilitates the cross-border mergers of UCITS, which will make it possible to increase the average size of European funds. In the same vein, UCITS IV allows for master-feeder structures, which have so far been specifically excluded due to fund diversification rules.[65] All these measures should allow for entity pooling, generate scale economies and thus contribute to a consolidation of the sector, which should serve the end-users of funds. UCITS IV further eases the cross-border marketing of UCITS by simplifying administrative procedures: there will be immediate market access once the authorisation has been granted by the country of

---

[64] Other forms of portfolio management, i.e. the management of pension fund portfolios or those of individuals, are presented as a form of derogation from the central objective of the Directive, which is the management of investment funds as authorised under the Directive (Art. 5).

[65] A feeder UCITS is a UCITS or an investment compartment thereof that invests at least 85% of its assets in one other UCITS, called the master UCITS.

origin of the UCITS. The host country will be able to monitor the commercial documents but not block access to the market.

UCITS IV also improves investor information by creating a standardised summary information document: 'key investor information' (KII). This should make it easier for the consumer to understand the product. The KII will replace the simplified prospectus of UCITS III.

Notwithstanding the recent decline, UCITS is considered a European regulatory success and a worldwide brand. It started from a limited basis in 1985, covering product rules for equity, bond and money market funds, which remain intact in the latest amendments, although the scope of the directive has been considerably enlarged. The UCITS III Product Directive signalled a first expansion, and allowed for funds investing in money market instruments, bank deposits, financial derivatives, index funds, units of other UCITS and non-UCITS funds (funds of funds).

More recently, a new regulatory initiative was launched by the European Commission[66] to cover the packaged retail investment products (PRIPS), which offer exposure to underlying financial assets in a packaged form and which modify that exposure compared with direct holdings. If well designed in terms of investor protection, such a regulatory initiative is expected to foster growth in this market.

Finally it is also important to mention the role of the Investor Compensation Scheme (ICS).[67] The ICS was adopted in 1997 to complement the Investment Services Directive,[68] which has since been replaced by MiFID.[69] The ICS has provided investors with some protection through the possibility to be compensated in specific circumstances where the investment firm is unable to return the money or the financial instruments that it holds on the client's behalf. In the aftermath of the crisis, this

---

[66] Consultation was held by the Commission services on the legislative steps for the PRIPS Initiative, January 2011.

[67] See Directive 97/9/EC of the European Parliament and of the Council of 3 March 1997 on investor compensation schemes, OJ L 84, 26.3.1997, p. 22.

[68] Refer to Council Directive 93/22/EEC of 10 May 1993 on investment services in the securities field, OJ L 141, 11.6.1993, pp. 27–46.

[69] See Directive 2004/39/EC of the European Parliament and the Council of 21 April 2004 on markets in financial instruments amending Council Directives 85/611/EEC and 93/6/EEC and Directive 2000/12/EC of the European Parliament and of the Council and repealing Council Directive 93/22/EEC, OJ L 145/1, 30.4.2004, pp. 1–44.

Directive was revisited to better protect investors (e.g. the increase of the level of compensation from €20,000 to €50,000 and other refinements related to the funding principles, the borrowing last resort mechanisms among national schemes, co-insurance, payout delays and investor information) and to better align itself with the MiFID provisions. The Directive may have to be revisited again in the wake of the adoption of the PRIPS Directive, which may eventually reopen the debate about the relevance of an EU solution to protect investors in the EU.

2.4   Overall assessment

Tables 4 and 5 provide a summarised assessment of the current market and regulatory status and the proposed way forward in the retail financial services market in Europe.

Table 4. Policy assessment and way forward in retail financial services

Area	Diagnosis	Latest policy/market initiatives	Achievements/ limits	Way forward
Payments	Very low cross-border transactions	Payment Service Directive (PSD)	Legal harmonisation of payment market Partial implementation of SEPA	Continuous monitoring (implementation of the PSD and pricing transparency) is required
Current accounts	Large divergence in pricing Low transparency and high level of complexity	Self-regulation	Low customer mobility and very high switching costs in general Current account is tied with other retail financial services (mortgage and consumer credit)	
Consumer credit	Growth in national markets	Consumer Credit Directive		Responsible lending rules
Mortgage credit	Cross-border supply is limited	Forthcoming measures on mortgage credit		More transparency and simplicity of offers

Table 4. cont'd

Retail investments	Cross-border supply growth of UCITS	UCITS I, II, III, IV PRIPS	Simplification of prospectus Links with MiFID (investor protection)	Restrictions on complex and risky products should be considered

Source: Author's compilation.

Table 5. Proposed comprehensive framework to regulate retail financial services

Area/rules	Disclosure of costs and risks **Availability and comparability of information**	Consumer protection **Enforcement of regulation on unfair commercial practices** **Redress (collective and individual)**	Protection in case of crisis **Deposit guarantee schemes** **Investment compensation schemes**
Current accounts/payments/savings	Yes	Yes	Yes
Consumer credit	Yes	Yes	n.a.
Mortgage credit	Yes	Yes	n.a.
UCITS	Yes	Yes	Yes
PRIPS	Yes	Yes	Yes*

* Not yet considered.

Source: Author's compilation.

3. Challenges ahead

To promote the internal market for retail financial services, it is essential to respond to the related political challenges that lie ahead in ensuring financial safety for retail consumers and to enhance consumer protection at the EU level.

3.1 Financial safety

One specific aspect of the financial safety net that has been in the spotlight concerns the deposit guarantee schemes – which provide protection for retail depositors so that if a credit institution fails, they are able to recover at least a portion of their bank deposits. Deposit guarantee schemes also serve to prevent runs on banks, and if properly designed, to facilitate bank closures. The run on the British bank Northern Rock in September 2008 was clear evidence of the failure of such schemes to fulfil one of the aims. This leads us to consider how to improve their institutional and operational design.

The 1994 Directive (94/19/EC) on deposit guarantee schemes provided a minimum harmonisation background for establishing deposit-guarantee schemes in the member states. While the criteria used in the directive were generally harmonised in terms of the scope (the exclusion of the interbank and corporate deposits) and the minimum coverage (fixed at €20,000 per person per bank), they fell short of ensuring a sound deposit-guarantee system in Europe. Indeed, the directive was implemented unevenly in the member states as a result of divergent interpretations of its provisions. There are clear differences in the legal frameworks, the administration of the schemes, the extent of coverage, the co-insurance practices and the sources of funding. In light of the continuing trends of cross-border banking these divergences in implementation present major challenges in terms of protecting retail banking customers. While foreign branches of EU banks are covered by the home deposit-guarantee scheme, foreign subsidiaries of EU banks are covered by the host deposit-guarantee scheme. The home and host schemes can be intrinsically different, and depositors are not necessarily aware of such differences and in the majority of the cases are not protected evenly. The situation grows more complex in the case of branches of non-EU banks and in countries where no deposit guarantee scheme exists. Not only does this raise competitive considerations and can it be the source of potential conflicts of interest between the host and the home countries' authorities, but it also adds further confusion and complications for depositors, particularly if a bank failure occurs.

These limitations were acknowledged by the European Commission in a Communication[70] in November 2006, less than a year before the eruption of the crisis. The conclusions concurred that changes should not be made to the directive, but instead work should focus on providing some interpretative guidance and recommendations on the main aspects of the directive.[71]

The financial crisis has put into doubt the adequacy of the existing national schemes and the wisdom of the European Commission's decision not to amend the directive earlier, while putting pressure on governments in the member states to take individual, uncoordinated actions to help restore confidence in their domestic markets. These individual actions have prompted EU policy-makers to revise the original directive to prevent any competitive distortions. Amendments have since been put forward, more importantly to reassure depositors than to promote the convergence of deposit guarantee schemes. The amendments entail revisions in three key areas: a) an increase of the minimum coverage level (from a minimum of €20,000 to at least €50,000 and within a further year to at least €100,000),[72] b)

---

[70] See European Commission (2006e) (http://ec.europa.eu/internal_market/bank/docs/guarantee/comm9419_en.pdf).

[71] More specifically, it would include the definition of deposits and scope of coverage, co-insurance, topping-up arrangements, the exchange of information requirements, the risk-based contributions to deposit guarantee schemes (DGS), the transferability/refundability of DGS contributions, consumer information and advertising.

[72] In the compromise package that the Council published on 24 November 2008, which was agreed on 2 December 2008, changes were introduced to the

a reduction of the payout delay to a maximum of three days and c) the termination of co-insurance.

The 2008 amendments to Directive 94/19/EC provide useful lessons for a fundamental review of the adequacy of the existing schemes and for the discussion of possible improvements to level the playing field in Europe[73] and ensure that European retail banking customers enjoy the same level of protection within the internal market. So far, this is not yet the case; instead, the fragmentation of deposit insurance in Europe and the low level of customer awareness act as impediments to further integration in the retail banking market.

3.2   Consumer protection

As it stands, markets have a strong local orientation and removing important consumer-protection measures in a well-intended effort to dismantle perceived barriers to the single market risks regulatory arbitrage. Regulatory standards could fall to the lowest common denominator, which would ultimately undermine the single market. A maximum harmonisation approach has limited use in this regard and the Commission must commit to ensuring that robust and consistent minimum standards exist in relation to the provision of information; the quality of financial advice; regulations, legal protection and collective redress; and professional standards. Other approaches, such as the 28th regime, may seem unrealistic, as in the latter case it will certainly face political resistance (see appendix 4). It is self-evident that if the single market is to stand any chance of developing as envisaged, i.e. towards more integration in retail financial services markets, then consumer confidence in these markets is a prerequisite. It follows that this confidence depends on consumers being 1) financially educated and 2) protected through adequately enforced regulations, and having easy access to redress along with a strong voice in policy-making.

Commission's original proposal with respect to coverage levels. The timeline for increasing the coverage to €100,000 was extended by two years (from 31 December 2009 to 31 December 2011), subject to a report by the European Commission to evaluate the impact of such an increase and the necessity for this amount to become a harmonised coverage level in the Community.

[73] See Ayadi and Lastra (2010).

Financial education is useful and if carried out properly, can be beneficial. The challenge is to determine the extent of financial capability that an average consumer should be expected to have to be able to behave rationally in the complex financial market. Still, it should be born in mind that financial literacy cannot replace well-enforced regulations and adequate consumer protection rules to ensure access, fair play and adequate information for consumers.

Indeed, implementing and enforcing existing directives (for example, those on Consumer Credit and Undertakings in Collective Investments in Transferable Securities, UCITS) and ensuring regulatory consistency in other areas, such as mortgage credit and packaged retail investment products, will not only help to achieve regulatory coherence and convergence but most importantly will enhance market confidence. Regulation must be enforced, as is the case for competition policy. Competition authorities have the power to levy substantial fines on market participants who breach competition law. This means that firms' senior management, and crucially institutional investors,[74] are very aware of the risks of breaching competition law, which has a very powerful disciplining effect on corporate behaviour. The approach to enforcing regulation needs to be revisited and complemented by a credible system of sanctions if rules are breached. The role of the new European Supervisory Authorities is paramount to achieve this.

In addition, consumers must have access to the necessary and relevant information on all retail financial products supplied by financial services providers in the 27 member states to allow them to make informed, effective choices and decisions. If access to information is to be effective as a policy tool, it is important that the information disclosed to consumers is easily available, consistent, easily understandable and comparable, and that it covers the *risks, costs, features, terms and conditions,* and *redress* associated with the product and service. As soon as regulatory and consumer policy frameworks are maximally harmonised, an observatory of retail financial services is to be established to improve transparency and to ensure comparability among products and services. On the supply side, financial institutions, advisers/intermediaries and other players should be required to operate with a generally high duty of care in assessing consumers' needs and level of financial sophistication (where possible), so that appropriate

---

[74] One can also add other influential players, such as brokers and company analysts.

advice and recommendations are given. Mis-selling, unduly high prices, unfair commercial practices and the provision of improper information to customers must be banned and legally sanctioned. The sales rules under the Markets in Financial Instruments and the Insurance Mediation Directives must be properly enforced. An annual consumer satisfaction barometer should be part of the strategies of financial providers and must become part of their annual reports. All in all, an EU ethical code of conduct should be agreed and enforced by the profession in close consultation with consumer organisations. Responsibility for enforcing the code should be taken by the boards. Consumer satisfaction is as important as that of other stakeholders. Furthermore, the Commission should produce clear guidelines about i) consumer needs assessments (for example, information gathering, transparency level and adequacy of financial services) and ii) recognised professional standards to ensure that intermediaries/advisers apply consistently high standards in their domestic and cross-border services.

Finally, the interests of end-users of financial services (consumers, pensioners, small enterprises, retail investors and so forth) must be better represented at the EU level. It is therefore critical that the EU increases the resources available to advocates of end-users and develops ideas on how to create a more level playing field during the policy-making process in future. Capacity building could be complemented by the set-up of a European consumer protection agency in the medium term when evidence of more retail financial market integration is apparent. Its mandate would be to protect European end-users from deceptive practices by the financial industry and to enforce relevant regulations in retail financial services (currently under the mandate of the three European Supervisory Authorities). The agency should be funded under the EU's budget.

BIBLIOGRAPHY

Adam, K., T. Jappelli, A. Menichini, M. Padula and M. Pagano (2002), *Analyse, compare, and apply alternative indicators and monitoring methodologies to measure the evolution of capital market integration in the European Union*, Working Paper, Centre for Studies in Economics and Finance, University of Salerno.

Alter-EU (2009), *A captive Commission: The role of the financial industry in shaping EU regulation*, Alter-EU, Brussels (http://www.alter-eu.org/sites/default/files/documents/expertgroupsreport.pdf).

AT Kearney (2008), *The SEPA shake-out: Challenges in cards and payments*, AT Kearney, Chicago (http://www.atkearney.com/images/global/pdf/SEPAShake-Out.pdf).

Ayadi, R. (2006), "Les fusions et Acquisitions bancaires européennes et leurs performances", Thèse de Doctorat, Université Paris Dauphine, Septembre.

Ayadi, R., and G. Pujals (2004), *Banking consolidation in the EU: Overview and prospects*, CEPS Research Report on Finance and Banking No. 34, Centre for European Policy Studies, Brussels, April.

Ayadi, R. and J. Rodkiewicz (2008), *Tackling financial exclusion in Europe: The market response*, Financial Institutions and Prudential Policy Unit, Centre for European Policy Studies, Brussels (http://www.ecosocdoc.be/static/module/bibliographyDocument/document/001/384.pdf).

Ayadi, R. and R. Lastra (2010), *Crisis Management at Cross-Roads: Proposals for Reforming Deposit Guarantee Schemes in Europe*, SUERF Study 2010, European Money and Finance Forum, Vienna (http://www.suerf.org/download/studies/study20101.pdf).

Ayadi, R., D.T. Llewelyn, R.H. Schmidt, E. Arbak and W.P.D. Groen (2010), *Investigating Diversity in the Banking Sector in Europe: Key Developments, Performance and Role of Cooperative Banks*, Centre for European Policy Studies, Brussels.

Ayadi, R., R.H. Schmidt, S. Carbo Valverde, E. Arbak and F. Rodriguez Fernandez (2009), *Investigating Diversity in the Banking Sector in Europe: The Performance and Role of Savings Banks*, Centre for European Policy Studies (CEPS), Brussels.

Baltzer, M., L. Cappiello, R.A. De Santis and S. Manganelli (2008), *Measuring financial integration in new EU Member States*, ECB Occasional Paper Series No. 81, ECB, Frankfurt, March (http://www.ecb.int/pub/pdf/scpops/ecbocp81.pdf).

Bank for International Settlements (BIS), Basel Committee on Banking Supervision (2004), *International Convergence of Capital Measurement and Capital Standards: A Revised Framework*, BIS, Basel, June (http://www.bis.org/publ/bcbs107.pdf?noframes=1).

Bikker, J.A., L. Spierdijk and P. Finnie (2006), *The impact of bank size on market power*, DNB Working Paper No. 120, DNB, Amsterdam.

Berger, A.N., R. DeYoung and G.F. Udell (2000), "Efficiency Barriers to the Consolidation of the European Financial Services Industry", *European Financial Management,* Vol. 6 (http://www.federalreserve.gov/PUBS/FEDS/2000/200037/200037pap.pdf).

Brada, J.C., A.M. Kutan and S. Zhou (2005), "Real and monetary convergence within the European Union and between the European Union and candidate countries: A rolling cointegration approach", *Journal of Banking and Finance*, Vol. 29, No. 1, pp. 249–70.

Capgemini (2008), *World Retail Banking Report*, Capgemini, Woking (http://www.at.capgemini.com/m/at/tl/World_Retail_Banking_Report_2008.pdf).

Carbó, S., E.P.M Gardener and P. Molyneux (2005), *Financial exclusion*, Basingstoke: Palgrave Macmillan.

Casu, B. and C. Girardone (2002), *Efficiency of Large Banks in the Single European Market*, Working Paper, University of Wales, Bangor, and Middlesex University.

————— (2007), *Does competition lead to efficiency? The case of EU commercial banks*, Discussion Paper No. 07–01, Essex University.

Centre for European Policy Studies (CEPS) (2008), *Corporate taxation and the European Company Statute*, CEPS Task Force Report, Rapporteur: E. Arbak, CEPS, Brussels, January.

Centre for European Policy Studies (CEPS) and European Credit Research Institute (ECRI) (2011), *A new retail credit regime for Europe: Setting the right priorities*, Task Force Report, CEPS, Brussels (forthcoming).

Commission of the European Communities (1992), *Report of the Committee of Independent Experts on Company Taxation*, Brussels.

Committee of European Insurance and Occupational Pensions Supervisors (CEIOPS) (2007), *Report on Financial Conditions and Financial Stability in the European Insurance Occupational Pension Fund Sector 2006-2007 (Risk Update)*, CEIOPS, Frankfurt.

Consumer Policy Evaluation Consortium (2008), *Preparing the Monitoring of the Impact of the Single Euro Payment Area (SEPA) on Consumers*, DG Health and Consumer Protection, European Commission, Brussels (http://ec.europa.eu/consumers/rights/docs/SEPA_monitoring_ study.pdf).

Delgado, J. (2006), "Single market trails home bias", Policy Brief 2006/05, Bruegel, Brussels, October.

Dermine, J. (2006), "European banking integration: Don't put the cart before the horse", *Financial Markets, Institutions & Instruments*, Vol. 15, No. 2, pp. 57–106.

Endres, D., A. Oestreicher, W. Scheffler and C. Spengel (2007), *The determination of corporate taxable income in the EU member states*, Alphen aan den Rijn: Kluwer Law International.

Ernst & Young (2007), *2007-2008 Global Transfer Pricing Survey*, Ernst & Young, London.

European Banking Federation (EBF) (2007), *Report on Integration of European Financial Services Markets*, EBF, Brussels.

European Banking Industry Committee (EBIC) (2009), *Third Progress Report on Implementation in the EU*, EBIC, Brussels, April.

European Funds & Asset Management Association (Efama) (2009), "Trends in the European Investment Fund Industry in the Third Quarter of 2009", Efama, Brussels.

European Central Bank (ECB) (2007), *EU banking structures*, ECB, Frankfurt, October (http://www.ecb.int/pub/pdf/other/eubankingstructures 2007en.pdf).

———— (2008), *Blue Book*, ECB, Frankfurt (http://www.ecb.int/paym/ market/blue/html/index.en.html).

——————— (2010), *Financial integration in Europe*, ECB, Frankfurt, April (http://www.ecb.int/pub/pdf/other/financialintegrationineurope20 1004en.pdf).

European Commission (2001), Communication, Towards an Internal Market without tax obstacles: A strategy for providing companies with a consolidated corporate tax base for their EU-wide activities, COM(2001) 582, European Commission, Brussels, 23 October.

——————— (2004a), *Financial Integration Monitor 2004*, Commission Staff Working Document, SEC(2004) 559, DG Internal Market, European Commission, Brussels (http://ec.europa.eu/internal_market/ finances/docs/cross-sector/fin-integration/sec-2004-559_en.pdf).

——————— (2004b), *An assessment of the extent of an identified need for simplified, standard financial services products*, Report prepared for the European Commission, Charles River Associates, SANCO/2003/B4/001, Brussels (http://ec.europa.eu/consumers/ cons_int/fina_serv/cons_experiences/cra-simplified-products-main-report.pdf).

——————— (2004c), *European Tax Survey*, Taxation Papers, Working Paper No. 3/2004, DG Taxation and Customs Union, Brussels (http://ec.europa.eu/taxation_customs/resources/documents/tax_s urvey.pdf).

——————— (2005a), *Financial Integration Monitor 2005*, Commission Staff Working Document, SEC(2005) 927, DG Internal Market, European Commission, Brussels (http://ec.europa.eu/internal_market/ finances/docs/cross-sector/fin-integration/050708fim.pdf).

——————— (2005b), *Public Opinion in Europe on Financial Services*, Special Eurobarometer 230, European Commission, Brussels (http://ec.europa.eu/consumers/cons_int/fina_serv/cons_experien ces/report_eurobarometer63-2_en.pdf).

——————— (2005c), *The Costs and Benefits of Integration of EU Mortgage Markets*, Report for DG Internal Market and Services, London Economics.

——————— (2005d), *White Paper: Financial Services Policy 2005-2010*, COM(2009) 629 final, European Commission, Brussels (http://eur-lex.europa.eu/LexUriServ/site/en/com/2005/com2005_0629en01. pdf).

—————— (2005e), *Cross-border consolidation in the financial sector*, SEC(2005) 1398, European Commission, Brussels, 26 October.

—————— (2005f) *Public opinion in Europe on financial services*, Special Eurobarometer, European Commission, Brussels, September.

—————— (2006a), *Financial Integration Monitor 2006*, Commission Staff Working Document, SEC(2006) 1057, DG Internal Market, European Commission, Brussels (http://ec.europa.eu/internal_market/finances/docs/cross-sector/fin-integration/060728fim_en.pdf).

—————— (2006b), *Interim Report II: Current Accounts and Related Services, Sector Inquiry under Article 17, Regulation 1/2003 on Retail Banking*, European Commission, Brussels, 17 July.

—————— (2006c), Communication on tax treatment of losses in cross-border situations, COM(2006) 824, European Commission, Brussels, 19 December.

—————— (2006d), Communication on exit taxation and the need for coordination of member states' tax policies, COM(2006) 825 final, European Commission, Brussels, 19 December.

—————— (2006e), Communication concerning the review of Directive 94/19/EC on Deposit Guarantee Schemes, European Commission, Brussels (http://ec.europa.eu/internal_market/bank/docs/guarantee/comm9419_en.pdf).

—————— (2007a), *European Financial Integration Report 2007*, Commission Staff Working Document, SEC(2007) 1696, DG Internal Market, European Commission, Brussels (http://ec.europa.eu/internal_market/finances/docs/cross-sector/fin-integration/efir_report_2007_en.pdf).

—————— (2007b), *Report on the retail banking sector inquiry*, Commission Staff Working Document, SEC(2007) 106, European Commission, Brussels, 31 January (http://ec.europa.eu/competition/sectors/financial_services/inquiries/sec_2007_106.pdf).

—————— (2007c), *The EU market for consumer long-term retail savings vehicles comparative analysis of products, market structure, costs, distribution systems and consumer saving patters*, Report for the European Commission, BME Consulting, Brussels, (http://ec.europa.eu/internal_market/finances/docs/cross-sector/study_en.pdf).

————— (2007d), "Direct taxation: Infringement proceeding against Germany for its discriminatory rules applied to cross-border loss offset", Press Release IP/07/1547, European Commission, Brussels, 18 October.

————— (2007e), Communication amending Directive 2006/112/EC on the common system of value added tax, as regards the treatment of insurance and financial services, COM(2007) 747, European Commission, Brussels, 28 November.

————— (2007f), Green Paper on Retail Financial Services in the Single Market, COM(2007) 226 final, European Commission, Brussels, 30 April.

————— (2007g), *White Paper on the Integration of EU Mortgage Credit Markets*, COM(2007) 807 final, European Commission, Brussels, 18 December.

————— (2008a), *Preparing the Monitoring of the Impact of the Single Euro Payment Area (SEPA) on Consumers*, DG Health and Consumer Protection, European Commission, Brussels (http://ec.europa.eu/consumers/rights/docs/SEPA_monitoring_study.pdf).

————— (2008b), *EMU@10: Successes and challenges after 10 years of Economic and Monetary Union*, European Economy 2 (provisional version), European Commission, Brussels (http://ec.europa.eu/economy_finance/emu10/emu10report_en.pdf).

————— (2008c) "Corporate taxation: Commission requests the United Kingdom to properly implement an ECJ ruling on cross-border loss compensation", Press Release IP/08/1365, European Commission, Brussels, 18 September.

————— (2008d) "Direct taxes: The European Commission requests Spain to end discriminatory taxation of non-resident taxpayers", Press Release IP/08/1533, European Commission, Brussels, 16 October.

————— (2008e), *Impact Assessment*, Commission Staff Working Document, SEC(2007) 1554 final, European Commission, Brussels, 28 November.

————— (2008f), *Harmonisation of turnover taxes*, Background Paper requested by the Council Presidency, TAXUD/2414/08, European Commission, Brussels, 5 March.

——————— (2009a), *European Financial Integration Report 2009,* Commission Staff Working Document, SEC(2009) 1702 final, European Commission, Brussels (http://ec.europa.eu/internal_market/finances/docs/cross-sector/fin-integration/efir_report_2009_en.pdf).

——————— (2009b), *Report of the Expert Group on Credit Histories,* DG Internal Market and Services, European Commission, Brussels (http://ec.europa.eu/internal_market/consultations/docs/2009/credit_histories/egch_report_en.pdf).

——————— (2009c), *Study on Credit Intermediaries in the Internal Market,* DG Internal Market and Services, European Commission, Brussels (http://ec.europa.eu/internal_market/finservices-retail/docs/credit/credit_intermediaries_report_en.pdf).

——————— (2009d), *Data collection for prices of current accounts provided to consumers,* DG Health and Consumer Protection, European Commission, Brussels (http://ec.europa.eu/consumers/rights/docs/study_bank_fees_en.pdf).

——————— (2009e), *European Financial Integration Report 2008,* Commission Staff Working Document, SEC(2009) 19 final, European Commission, Brussels (http://ec.europa.eu/internal_market/finances/docs/cross-sector/fin-integration/efir_report_2008_en.pdf).

European Credit Research Institute (ECRI) (2009), *Lending to Households in Europe (1995-2008),* ECRI Statistical Package 2009, Centre for European Policy Studies, Brussels.

European Financial Services Round Table (EFR) (2005), *Pan-European Pension Plans: Deepening the concept,* EFR, Brussels.

Eurostat (2006), *Living conditions in Europe,* Eurostat Pocketbooks, Brussels.

FIN-USE Expert Forum of Financial Services Users (2007), *Response to the Green Paper on Retail Financial Services in the Single* Market, FIN-USE, European Commission, Brussels, 3 November.

Flood, R.P. and A.K. Rose (2004), *Financial integration: A new methodology and an illustration,* Working Paper 04/110, IMF, Washington, D.C.

Hollo, D. and M. Nagy (2006), *Bank Efficiency in the Enlarged European Union,* BIS Paper No. 28, BIS, Basel, pp. 217–35.

Huizinga, H. (2002), "A European VAT on financial services?", *Economic Policy,* Vol. 17, pp. 498-534.

International Bureau of Fiscal Documentation (IBFD) (2006), *VAT Survey Financial Services – Survey on the recovery of input VAT in the financial sector*, IBFD, Amsterdam, December.

Kasman, A. and C. Yildirim (2006), "Cost and profit efficiencies in transition banking: The case of new EU members", *Applied Economics*, Vol. 38, No. 9, pp. 1079–90.

Kleimeier, S. and H. Sander (2000), "Regionalisation versus globalisation in European financial market integration: Evidence from co-integration analysis", *Journal of Banking and Finance*, Vol. 24, No. 6, pp. 1005–43.

——————— (2003), "European financial market integration: Evidence on the emergence of a single eurozone retail banking market", *Research in Banking and Finance*, Vol. 3, pp. 13–91.

——————— (2006), "Regional versus global integration of Eurozone retail banking markets: Understanding the recent evidence from price-based integration measures", *Quarterly Review of Economics and Finance*, Vol. 46, No. 3, pp. 353–68.

——————— (2007), *Integrating Europe's retail banking markets: Where do we stand?*, CEPS Research Report on Finance and Banking, Centre for European Policy Studies, Brussels (http://www.ceps.eu/node/1378).

Lannoo, K. (2010), *Regulatory Challenges for the EU Asset Management Industry*, ECMI Policy Brief, Centre for European Policy Studies, Brussels (http://www.ceps.eu/ceps/download/3094).

Lenoir, N. (2007), *La Societas Europaea ou SE: Pour une citoyenneté européenne de l'entreprise*, Paris: La Documentation Française.

Mercer Oliver Wyman and European Mortgage Federation (2003), *Study on the Financial Integration of European Mortgage Markets*, Mercer Oliver Wyman and European Mortgage Federation, London and Brussels (http://www.nykredit.com/investorcom/ressourcer/dokumenter/pdf/Wymanreport.pdf).

Morgan Stanley & Co. International Ltd and Mercer Oliver Wyman (2005), *European Banking Consolidation*, Morgan Stanley and Mercer Oliver Wyman, London, February.

Organisation for Economic Co-operation and Development (OECD) (2005), *Model Tax Convention on Income and on Capital*, OECD, Paris.

PricewaterhouseCoopers (PwC) (2006), *Study to Increase the Understanding of the Economic Effects of the VAT Exemption for Financial and Insurance Services*, Commissioned by the European Commission, PwC, London.

Renda, A., R. Ayadi, M. Lamandini, S. Cheliout, D. Mykolaitis, A. Naouar, D. Valiante, D. Spaey and S. Barel (2009), *Tying and other potentially unfair practices*, Report prepared for DG Markt/2008/04/H–24/11/2009, Centre for European Policy Studies, Brussels.

UniCredit Group (2008), *CEE Banking – Still the right bet*, UniCredit Group CEE Research Network, July.

Vajanne, L. (2007), *Integration in euro area banking markets – Convergence of credit interest rates*, Bank of Finland Research Discussion Papers, Bank of Finland, Helsinki (http://www.bof.fi/NR/rdonlyres/DF1FAB26-F911-4796-9E71-8084D0462A7F/0/0727netti.pdf).

Walkner, C. and J.P. Raes (2005), *Integration and consolidation in EU banking – An unfinished business*, European Economy Paper No. 226, DG Economic and Monetary Affairs, European Commission, Brussels, April, pp. 1–48.

Weill, L. (2009), "Convergence in banking efficiency across European countries", *Journal of International Financial Markets, Institutions and Money*, Vol. 19, No. 5, pp. 818–33.

Yoo, K.-Y. and A. De Serres (2004), *Tax Treatment of Private Pension Savings in OECD Countries and the Net Tax Cost Per Unit of Contribution to Tax-favoured Schemes*, OECD Working Paper No. 406, OECD, Paris.

Zentrum für Europäische Wirtschaftsforschung GmbH (ZEW) (2006), *Current Trends in the European Asset Management Industry Lot 1*, ZEW, Mannheim (http://ec.europa.eu/internal_market/investment/docs/other_docs/report_en.pdf).

APPENDIX 1. MAJOR OBSTACLES TO CROSS-BORDER CONSOLIDATION

In 2005, the European Commission conducted a survey (European Commission, 2005e) to assess the extent of unjustified obstacles to cross-border consolidation. The results confirmed the existence of significant obstacles that prevent a full exploitation of scale economies in the internal market. In other words, EU financial institutions fail to extract the benefits of cross-border fixed-cost synergies, especially when compared with potential cost synergies resulting from domestic transactions.[75] The reasons behind the lack of a business rationale for cross-border consolidation are threefold:

1)   Supervisory and reporting matters for cross-border institutions

Obstacles related to multiple supervisory requirements for cross-border activities ranked in first position as an explanation for the lack of fixed-cost synergies for the large and very large institutions. More than 90% of the large institutions (assets of between €1 billion and €100 billion) pointed to the constraints of multiple reporting requirements and divergence of supervisory practices.[76] For the very large institutions (assets of over €100 billion) this ranked second (with more than 30% of the respondents in this category), behind the overarching issue of non-overlapping fixed costs (around 55%). It ranked in the first position for smaller institutions. These results are not surprising, since most of the very large institutions already have cross-border businesses, and should therefore already be familiar with the supervision of cross-border activities.

---

[75] It is interesting to note that the share of fixed costs in total costs has markedly increased in the financial sector over the last few years. For instance, one study estimates that, in banking, the proportion of fixed costs has increased from 10-15% in the early 1990s to about 25-30% today (see the study, *European Banking Consolidation* by Morgan Stanley & Co. International Ltd and Mercer Oliver Wyman, 2005).

[76] Note that respondents were able to select more than one answer.

Because of multiple reporting requirements by different national authorities, it is more difficult for a cross-border company to streamline its back-office operations. By contrast, within a domestic group, those functions can be more easily combined, leading to potentially greater business efficiency.

2) Legal and tax impediments to corporate expansion and reorganisation

Another reason identified for a lack of cross-border synergies is that it is difficult to reorganise business operations on a cross-border basis, as one would do in a domestic group.

Among the list of potential obstacles to cross-border reorganisation, nearly all the financial institutions that took part in the survey identified the taxation on dividends as a significant one. Commercial banks also pointed at other obstacles that could impede companies from streamlining and reorganising their business functions on a cross-border basis: differences in employment legislation (in third position, with around 30% of the respondents in this category), legal structures of the companies and possible risks of double taxation resulting from exit taxes on capital gains. The issue of inter-group VAT was also among the obstacles most often mentioned. Some of these issues are specific to the financial sector, such as the problem of inter-group VAT, due to its partial non-recoverability, and also the variations in the legal structures of companies, which are sometimes more constraining in the financial sector than in other economic sectors. Other obstacles are not specific to the financial sector, but they add to the specific ones and further reduce the economic attractiveness of a cross-border deal.

3) Difficulties in selling the same products across countries

Small and medium-sized institutions primarily identified product-related obstacles, notably the differences in tax treatment (either discriminatory or resulting from specific domestic tax breaks – more than 80% of small institutions and around 45% of medium-sized institutions). Uncertainties as to the VAT treatment applicable in other member states were also seen as an obstacle.

More generally, the smaller institutions pointed to the disparities among countries in the product mix, which limit the scope for cross-border cost synergies. As explained above, these differences may be partially explained by differences in tax regimes. More deeply rooted factors, such as history (consumers being used to specific products) or culture (especially linguistic considerations) may also come into play. The survey results additionally identified legal factors, such as divergent consumer protection rules or differences in private law.

Other obstacles relate to environmental factors that discourage or block cross-border transactions, such as political interference in the process and misuse of supervisory powers. These factors create an unfavourable environment for cross-border transactions, which may dissuade market participants from launching a cross-border bid or block them once they have launched one.

For instance, the following issues are mentioned in the European Commission's (2005e) survey, more often by companies having past experience in cross-border M&As: political interference (nearly 30%), misuse of supervisory powers (nearly 20%), or limits or controls on foreign participation (nearly 20%). Similarly, political interference ranks fourth among the companies having been blocked in the process of a cross-border transaction.

It is difficult to characterise these obstacles with certitude, as they may take very different forms, from legal measures hampering or preventing acquisitions to direct political intervention in the transaction process, indirect influence at the various decision-making levels, or abuse of otherwise legitimate legal provisions or discretionary powers.

Industry conveyed a message that these obstacles can only be tackled with the strong political will to i) establish a cross-border regulatory framework for financial institutions, with a strong lead supervisor model; ii) build on integrated infrastructures, such as SEPA and clearing and settlement systems; iii) allow optimal cross-border organisation (outsourcing, tax penalties (VAT), transfer pricing and exit tax); and iv) harmonise consumer protection rules.

Following the 2005 Commission survey, policy initiatives were taken to improve the prudential assessment process for M&As in financial services. These initiatives included the introduction of a transparent notification and decision-making process; shorter deadlines during the examination process; a limited use of stopping-of-the-clock under clear and specific conditions; and clarified and fully harmonised criteria to assess the suitability of the acquirer throughout. In March 2007, the related amendments to the following directives were agreed: the Banking Directive (2006/48/EC), the Third Non-Life Insurance Directive (92/49/EEC), the Recast Life Assurance Directive (2002/83/EC), the Reinsurance Directive (2005/68/EC) and the Directive on Markets in Financial Instruments (2006/48/EC).

APPENDIX 2.

TAX IMPEDIMENTS TO FINANCIAL MARKET INTEGRATION

Fiscal measures would seem to be among the most crucial elements that hamper the integration of the financial sector in the EU. A common factor is that cross-border groups are put in a more disadvantageous position than domestic groups because of the application of a certain fiscal regime. Another commonality is the way that the EU has had to respond with these problems, which has led to a patchy and case-by-case response to the tax impediments standing in the way of financial market integration. Owing to the particularities of EU tax policy, where Council decisions can only be adopted by a unanimous vote, the main policy tools are the European Commission's infringement procedures or rulings in cases brought before the European Court of Justice (ECJ). Far from addressing the issues in a systematic manner, these actions lead to a patchy line of defence against the tax obstacles.

Becoming a cross-border group is associated with a number of problems that would not arise for a domestic firm. One of these issues is a multi-national group's inability to offset losses incurred in one country from profits earned in another. Since losses are not taxable, loss offsetting actually reduces a group's total taxable income and tax obligations. Most EU member states recognise domestic tax grouping, which allows loss offsetting for qualified groups of firms within the same member state.[77] Yet such an option is often not available on a cross-border basis.[78] In consequence, multinational groups within the EU may at times lack the tax advantages available to purely domestic groups.

---

[77] Currently, Belgium, the Czech Republic, Estonia, Greece, Hungary, Lithuania and Slovakia are among the EU member states that do not have a group taxation regime, enabling qualifying groups to compute their tax liabilities on a combined and consolidated basis (Endres et al., 2007, Table 90).

[78] Non-resident subsidiaries can be a part of a tax group in Austria, Denmark, France and Italy (Endres et al., 2007, Table 94).

The European Commission adopted a Communication in 2006 showing its willingness to end the discriminatory treatment of losses emanating from a foreign group entity.[79] Member states were urged to review their tax systems in compliance with the freedom of establishment principle provided for by the EC Treaty. Since then, the Commission has initiated a number of infringement procedures by requesting various member states to allow cross-border loss offsetting.[80, 81]

A closely related issue to loss offsetting stems from compliance costs arising from anti-transfer pricing rules. Tax authorities around the world rely on a variety of mechanisms to ensure that the pricing of these transactions actually reflects the underlying value of the good or service provided.[82] The concern is that by applying an artificially high price,

---

[79] The Communication (COM(2006) 824) and its technical annexes (SEC(2006) 1690) were published on 19 December 2006 (European Commission, 2006c). Among other things, the Communication highlighted the technical difficulties associated with the administrative delays arising from the cross-border transfers of losses. The Communication followed the ECJ's highly influential ruling in *Marks & Spencer plc v. David Halsey (Her Majesty's Inspector of Taxes)* (Case C-446/03 of 13 December 2005), where the Court ruled that the UK's ban on cross-border loss relief was disproportionate and asked for provisions to be set in place to grant relief for cross-border losses of a subsidiary established in another EU member state.

[80] Since 2006, the Commission has formally asked the UK and Germany to end the discriminatory rules applied to cross-border losses (see Press Release IP/08/1365 on the UK, European Commission, 2008c; and IP/07/1547 on Germany, European Commission, 2007d). In the German case, the proceedings were closed in May 2009 after Germany changed its legislation. As for the UK, the Commission's argument rested on the complaint that the UK had failed to properly implement the ECJ's 2005 ruling in the *Marks & Spencer* case.

[81] A more concrete solution is through the completion of the EU's common consolidated corporate tax base (CCCTB) project, which was set in motion in 2001 (COM(2001) 582 – see European Commission, 2001). The regime gives qualifying groups the option to pool their Community-wide profits. Once consolidated, the profits are shared among member states according to a set of apportionment rules, which are then subjected to taxes. The regime has not materialised, mostly owing to strong resistance from certain member states. For a more detailed discussion on how CCCTB could lift some of the tax barriers that impede the spread of cross-border firms within EU, see CEPS (2008).

[82] One of the most common means of enforcement is the *arm's length principle*. First proposed by the Organisation for Economic Cooperation and Development

multinational corporations can shift profits from high-tax jurisdictions to low-tax jurisdictions.[83] The mechanisms put in place to combat such practices generate significant compliance costs for all cross-border groups.[84] Purely domestic groups that operate within a single tax regime, however, are not subject to a similar scrutiny since shifting profits would not be beneficial.

Cross-border restructuring is also problematic when member states apply exit taxes on assets leaving a member state. By charging one-time taxes on departing assets, tax authorities effectively discriminate against cross-border structures and contradict the freedom of establishment and capital movement principles enshrined in the Treaty. Some illegitimate uses of exit taxes have been addressed by the 1990 Taxation of Mergers Directive (90/434/EEC).[85] In 2006, the Commission adopted a Communication[86] renewing its willingness to uproot the use of exit taxes during the restructuring of taxes. Since then, member states have either rescinded or have been asked by the Commission to abolish the use of exit taxes.[87]

(OECD, 2005), the principle requires that the intra-group transfers reflect the market prices upon which a pair of unrelated parties would have agreed.

[83] Indeed, transfer pricing can make certain types of cross-border structures more beneficial. For example, corporations can setup or acquire 'holding companies' in low-tax countries, which can be used to store the group's profits. These profits can then be redistributed within the group by dividend distributions, which are exempted from taxation in the destination (high-tax) countries through the Parent–Subsidiary Directive (2003/123/EC).

[84] According to a survey published by the European Commission (2004c), transfer pricing is an important obstacle to cross-border activity for over 70% of the respondents. Once again, CCCTB would make transfer pricing obsolete, as transfers would have no impact on the total pooled amount.

[85] See Council Directive 90/434/EEC of 23 July 1990 on the common system of taxation applicable to mergers, divisions, transfers of assets and exchanges of shares concerning companies of different Member States, OJ L 225, 20.8.1990.

[86] See COM(2006) 825 final (European Commission, 2006d).

[87] Most recently, the Commission has asked Sweden to change its tax provisions imposing an exit tax on companies leaving the country on 18 September 2008 (in Press Release IP/08/1533 – see European Commission, 2008d).

The differential tax treatment of dividends within the EU is another serious impediment to cross-border business, especially in the financial services sector.[88] In general, dividends are taxed twice; once through the corporate tax on profits, and a second time through the tax on shareholder earnings. Some member states address double taxation by granting the shareholders some form of relief.[89] One common mechanism is to impute credits based on taxes paid or withheld. In these cases, discrimination may arise from granting credits only for domestic dividends or by applying a higher withholding tax to foreign shareholders.[90] In either case, domestic distributions receive more relief than foreign distributions, leading to an obstacle to cross-border investment.

Several mechanisms have been put in place to address the differential treatment of cross-border dividends. A few countries maintain bilateral agreements (the so-called 'DTAs' or double tax agreements) that homogenise the taxation of dividends. More generally, the ECJ and the European Commission have acted to end the discriminatory treatment of dividends on the grounds that such practices do not comply with the principle of the free movement of capital set out in Article 56 of the EC Treaty. Since 2006, the European Commission has been very active in uprooting the discriminatory treatment of dividend payments to foreign corporations (including financial institutions such as pension funds) and has started legislative action against a number of countries, including Austria, Belgium, Finland, Germany, Spain, Italy, the Netherlands and Portugal. Several of these countries have been referred to the ECJ.[91]

A final challenge for financial integration stems from the way that exemptions have been granted under the Sixth VAT Directive of 1977

---

[88] The European Commission's survey (2005b) uncovered that the discriminatory treatment of dividend distributions is one of the major tax-related obstacles faced by financial institutions across Europe.

[89] Group distributions are, to a large extent, exempted from income taxation by the (amended) Parent–Subsidiary Directive (2003/123/EC).

[90] For the latter case, the discrimination may be direct, as in different withholding rates, or indirect, such as income tax credits based on withholding taxes paid.

[91] For more details on the Commission's actions, see the list of infringement cases on the European Commission's website, Taxation and Customs Union, "Infringement cases by policy area", 1 February 2011 (http://ec.europa.eu/taxation_customs/common/infringements/infringement_cases/bypolicy/index_en.htm#CompanyTax).

(77/388/EEC).[92] Under the directive, financial institutions have been exempt from VAT because of inherent difficulties in measuring value added in the sector. The exemption is treated differently by EU countries, leading to potential complexities, uncertainties and hidden costs. In effect, the exemption often means that taxes paid on inputs cannot be fully recovered. Indeed, a 2006 study found that the exemption was not applied homogenously, with the share of recovered VAT ranging from a low of 0% to a high of 74%.[93] Another study[94] showed that some member states allowed certain financial institutions the option of taxing certain transactions, leading to large discrepancies among member states in the way services are exempt.[95]

In responding to these challenges, in 2007 the Commission proposed a directive aimed at allowing financial institutions to tax their services.[96] In cross-border transactions, much like in domestic cases, the option to tax overcomes the non-recoverability of input taxes by allowing financial institutions to subject their services to VAT. The business clients of financial institutions may also redeem the taxes on purchased services, preventing the cascading effect and ensuring that tax costs do not inflate along the supply chain and across borders. Although the proposed directive on VAT taxation is a promising solution in principle, the Commission's impact assessment[97] found that the implementation of the option to tax will lead to consequential tax revenue losses as financial institutions cherry-pick between opting in and out of the VAT. Moreover, there may be "political/social sensitivities associated with taxing consumers" not considered by the assessment. Nevertheless, the Commission has shown its

---

[92] See the Sixth Council Directive *77/388/EEC* of 17 May 1977 on the harmonisation of the laws of the Member States relating to turnover taxes — Common system of value added tax: uniform basis of assessment (OJ L 145, 13.6.1977), which was transposed into national laws by 1 January 1978.

[93] See PwC (2006). The study covered a total 22 institutions, headquartered in 7 EU member states with subsidiaries in all of the 25 EU member states.

[94] See IBFD (2006).

[95] This right emanates from Art. 13(C)(b) of Sixth VAT Directive, which allows member states a right of option for taxation.

[96] The Commission's proposal for a directive (COM(2007) 747) to modernise the VAT was issued on 28 November 2007 (see European Commission, 2007e).

[97] See SEC(2007) 1554 (European Commission, 2008e).

preference for the opt-in clause as the closest solution to treating financial services.[98] Since 2008, the directive has been the subject of lengthy discussions at the Council, challenged by the arguments of several member states in line with the view that the changes may lead to substantial revenue losses, which has been a particularly divisive topic since the onset of the financial crisis.

---

[98] The Commission's position was also made explicit in the Commission's background paper requested by the Council presidency, TAXUD/2414/08 (European Commission, 2008f).

APPENDIX 3.
INTEGRATION IN MORTGAGE LOAN MARKETS – OBSTACLES AND SOLUTIONS

Table A3. Integration in mortgage loan markets – Obstacles and solutions

Problem areas	Cross-border activity	Product diversity	Consumer confidence	Customer mobility	Commission's related actions
Legislation					
Applicable law – uncertainty about the law applicable to mortgage contracts	X		X		Application of 'Rome I Convention' [a)] to mortgage contracts Application of rules from the country of property location to collateral
Pre-contractual information: • insufficient and complex information; • non-comparability of information (e.g. of the annual percentage rate of charge, APRC); • provision of information at different times (in advance or together with a binding offer); and • lack of credible monitoring and enforcement of information requirements for the code of conduct on home loans.	X		X	X	Completion of the revision of the European Standard Information Sheet Preparation of an APRC study Preparation of a cost-benefit analysis

Table A3. cont'd

Early repayment: • different rules on when and under what circumstances consumers can repay early; and • different rules on the compensation chargeable in the event of early repayment.	X	X	X	X	Assessment of policy options
Interest rate restrictions (to prevent exorbitant interest rates): • presence of caps (ceilings) on the level and variability of interest rates; and • restrictions on use of compound interest rates.	X	X			Preparation of a study on interest rate restrictions
Obligation to be a credit institution: requirement in some countries to become a credit institution in order to engage in mortgage lending and carry out day-to-day servicing of the mortgage loan.	X	X			Preparation of a study on non-credit institutions
Mortgage funding					Continuation of the work of the Mortgage Funding Expert Group Reception of market feedback on complex financial tools Feasibility study on the creation of an Expert Group on Securitisation

Table A3. cont'd

Mortgage funding (covered bonds – debt instruments secured by a cover pool of eligible assets, e.g. mortgage loans): • non-existent legal framework in some member states; and • collateral instrument limitations (regarding the eligibility of assets for covering covered bonds).	X	X			Carrying out an investigation into covered bond rules
Mortgage funding (residential mortgage-backed securities): • diversity and fragmentation of national securitisation frameworks; and • limits for UCITS (undertakings for collective investment in transferable securities) with regard to investments in the residential mortgage-backed securities of single, residential mortgage-backed securities issuers (Art. 22, UCITS Directive). [b]	X				
Mortgage funding (transferability of mortgage loan portfolios): • existence of the requirement for consent or notification of the borrower for assignment of the claim; and • requirement of registration for changes to the beneficiary of the collateral.	X	X			

Table A3. cont'd

Mortgage funding (reporting): • different levels of reporting across the EU; • lack of consistency in definitions across the EU.	X	X			
Mortgage funding (data protection): • uncertainty in the interpretation of the definition of 'personal data' in the Data Protection Directive; [c)] • the requirement of the borrower's consent as the legal basis for the processing of personal data.	X				
Mortgage funding (Basel II): [d)] • differences in interpretation and application of the Capital Requirements Directive [e)] (14.6.2006) across jurisdictions; and • uncertainty regarding the sunset clause for the eligibility of residential mortgage-backed securities tranches as cover assets for covered bonds.	X				
Infrastructure					
Credit registers: • restricted access to credit registers; • high cost of obtaining credit data; and • incomplete reporting.	X			X	Preparation of a study on credit registers Creation of the Expert Group on Credit Histories Carrying out an investigation into credit data rules

Table A3. cont'd

Land registration: • problems with the accessibility of land registers; • high cost and long duration of land registration procedures; • lack of completeness of the land register (certain charges imposed on real estate are not accurately reflected – the so-called 'hidden charges').	X			X	Recommendations on land registration, foreclosure and property valuation Presentation of scoreboards on land registration
Long forced-sale procedures	X				Recommendations on land registration, foreclosure and property valuation
Property valuation: • lack of reliable valuation standards (lack of common valuation principles, valuation methodologies and standards for the professional qualification of property valuers); and • difficulties in using the valuation report for a foreign property in relations with public authorities.	X				Recommendations on land registration, foreclosure and property valuation
Supply					
Product tying	X			X	Preparation of a study/investigation
Demand					
Financial education – insufficient levels of financial literacy			X		Communication on financial education (issued)

Table A3. cont'd

Supply and demand					
Product suitability: • insufficient or incorrect assessment of creditworthiness; and • the sub-optimal quality of advice.			X		Examination on responsible lending Preparation of policy options assessment Consultation of stakeholders on advice standards
Other					
Lack of standardised, comparable house price indices across the EU	X				

a) European Economic Community, Convention on the law applicable to contractual obligations, opened for signature in Rome on 19 June 1980 (http://europa.eu/scadplus/leg/en/lvb/l33109.htm).

b) Council of the European Union, Council Directive 85/611/EEC of 20 December 1985 on the coordination of laws, regulations and administrative provisions relating to undertakings for collective investment in transferable securities (UCITS) (http://eur-lex.europa.eu/LexUriServ/LexUriServ.do?uri=CELEX:%2001985L0611-20050413:EN:NOT), with further amending Directives (see http://ec.europa.eu/internal_market/investment/legal_texts/index_en.htm).

c) European Parliament and the Council of the European Union, Directive 95/46/EC of the European Parliament and of the Council of 24 October 1995 on the protection of individuals with regard to the processing of personal data and on the free movement of such data 95/46/EC (http://eur-lex.europa.eu/LexUriServ/LexUriServ.do?uri=CELEX:31995L0046:EN:HTML).

d) See BIS (2004). The purpose of Basel II is to make regulatory capital requirements for banks more risk-sensitive, encourage banks to improve their risk management processes and facilitate market discipline on banks.

e) The Capital Requirements Directive (CRD) comprises Directive 2006/48/EC of the European Parliament and of the Council of the European Union of 14 June 2006 relating to the taking up and pursuit of the business of credit institutions (recast) (http://eur-lex.europa.eu/LexUriServ/LexUriServ.do?uri=OJ:L:2006:177:0001:0001:EN:PDF) and Directive 2006/49/EC of the European Parliament and of the Council of 14 June 2006 on the capital adequacy of investment firms and credit institutions (recast) (http://eur-lex.europa.eu/LexUriServ/LexUriServ.do?uri=OJ:L:2006:177:0201:0201:EN:PDF).

Source: Author's compilation.

APPENDIX 4. THE 28TH REGIME

The so-called '28th regime', first proposed in 2003 by Eurofi and later considered by the European Financial Services Round Table is a set of optional measures for consumer protection in relation to financial products marketed across the EU. Therefore, an institution can choose to apply the 28th regime or continue to operate under the national laws. To prevent transposition divergences among different member states, the proposed scheme is to be established by means of an EU regulation.

In essence, the regime allows institutions to have access to the EU market without having to comply with the different consumer protection rules in each member state the product is offered. Service providers may also continue to operate under the host country rules. The new regime seeks to cut the compliance costs without giving rise to unnecessary implementation costs.

The European Commission's Green Paper on Retail Financial Services has suggested that the optional regime could be examined as a potential solution for the cross-border integration of financial services, particularly for savings and private pension schemes.[99] The European Parliament has supported the idea of assessing whether the proposed optional regime would help achieve that objective.[100]

Allowing foreign products to be provided in the domestic market is a touchy matter, whether it is accomplished by an optional scheme or by changing laws altogether. The effort could be comparable in its complexity to achieving full harmonisation across the EU. An over-prescriptive set of rules would not be preferable for some; in turn, some governments may be concerned that a less prescriptive regime would provide regulatory

---

[99] See the Green Paper, COM(2007) 226 final (European Commission, 2007f).

[100] The Parliament adopted a resolution supporting the Green Paper on retail financial services on 5 June 2008. In its adopted text (T6-0261/2008), the Parliament calls on the Commission to put forward a timeframe to investigate the feasibility of the optional regime and highlights that the new regime should not in any way become an obstacle to the development of new services and products.

arbitrage opportunities.[101] More generally, the optional scheme – much like a harmonised mandatory regime – may override national interests and may be politically undesirable for some member states.[102]

A likely candidate for disagreements is the fiscal treatment of pan-EU pensions under the 28th regime. The tax treatment of private pensions varies significantly across member states. For example, while France, Germany, Italy, Spain and the UK tax only the benefits (operating under the so-called 'EET' system),[103] smaller countries, such as Austria, Belgium, Czech Republic, Hungary, Luxembourg and Portugal, tax contributions (Yoo and De Serres, 2004). Unless a common ground is reached, the cross-border provision of pension services could lead to the double-taxation of benefits during the transfer of vested rights and additional administrative costs for corporations providing pension services under different tax systems.

An optional scheme may also provide member states insufficient incentives to fully implement it. Indeed, countries with a predominant concern to preserve their national interests would have little to lose if various elements of the optional regime were left out. This would not be the case under full harmonisation, which would replace national laws and in doing so create incentives to ensure full engagement.

In summary, the development of an alternative 28th regime may be lengthy and the take-up of the final product may be less than sufficient.

---

[101] A similar concern was raised by the Commission's Expert Forum of Financial Services Users (FIN-USE) in its response to the Commission's Green Paper (FIN-USE, 2007). According to the document detailing its response, care must be taken so that the regime does not become a *"Trojan Horse* designed to reduce the levels of consumer protection"* across the EU (p. 34, emphasis given in the original). The FIN-USE response is available on the European Commission's website (http://ec.europa.eu/internal_market/finservices-retail/docs/policy/gp_other_eu_finuse_en.pdf).

[102] In their responses to the Commission's Green Paper (COM(2007) 226 final), most member states have opposed the establishment of a 28th regime.

[103] The fiscal treatment of retirement savings schemes around the world is distinguished by how countries tax contributions, investment returns and retirement benefits, respectively. EET (exempt-exempt tax) implies that only the third item, benefits, is taxed while contributions and investment returns are exempt. TEE stands for a system that taxes contributions but holds interest earnings and final benefits exempt from taxation

If member states are unwilling to harmonise consumer protection rules for fear of diluting national laws, they would be equally reluctant to give the optional scheme a fair chance. A better approach for enhancing the integration of financial services across Europe may be pushing for full harmonisation in key areas and mutual recognition in the remaining areas.

APPENDIX 5.
PARTICIPATING COMPANIES AND ORGANISATIONS IN THE **CEPS-ECRI** TASK FORCE ON THE INTERNAL MARKET FOR RETAIL FINANCIAL SERVICES

AEGON Scottish Equitable
AG Insurance
APCO Worldwide
Banco Santander
BBVA
BNP Paribas Fortis Bank
BPCE – Banque Populaire Caisses d'Epargne
British Bankers' Association
Bundesministerium der Finanzen
CEA – European Insurance and Reinsurance Federation
Citi
Citigate Dewe Rogerson Public Policy
Clifford Chance LLP
Cologne University of Applied Sciences
Commerzbank AG
Credit Suisse Asia Pacific
Danish Bankers' Association (Finansradet)
Deutsche Börse AG
Deutsche Post AG
Energy Charter Secretariat
Ernst & Young Sweden LLP
Euro Alliance
EUROFI
Eurofinas/Leaseurope
European Banking Federation (EBF-FBE)
European Commission
European Federation of Building Societies

European Financial Services Round Table (EFR)
European Funds & Asset Management Association (Efama)
European Savings Banks Group-World Savings Banks Institute
Fédération Bancaire Française
Federation of Austrian Industry
Finance & Leasing Association
Financial Services Authority
FIN-USE
Fleishman-Hillard
Groupement des Cartes Bancaires
HBOS plc
Heilbronn Business School & LECG
Houston Consulting Europe
ING Group
Intesa Sanpaolo
KULeuven – Katholieke Universiteit Leuven
Lloyds TSB
Mastercard
McKinsey & Company
National Bank of Austria
Novo Nordisk
Nykredit Realkredit A/S
Organisation for Economic Cooperation and Development (OECD)
Postbank ING Group
PriceWaterhouseCoopers
SEB
The Global Consulting Group
University of Ljubljana
University of Maastricht
Uria Menendez
Visa Europe
Volkswagen AG
Western Union
White & Case